D0146832

Voice
and Crisis

Voice
and Crisis

Invocation in Milton's Poetry

WALTER SCHINDLER

Archon Books

1984

First published 1984 as an Archon Book,
an imprint of The Shoe String Press, Inc.,
995 Sherman Avenue, Hamden, Connecticut 06514

Printed in the United States of America

The paper in this book meets the guidelines for permanence
and durability of the Committee on Production Guidelines
for Book Longevity of the Council on Library Resources.

Library of Congress Cataloging in Publication Data.

Schindler, Walter, 1951—
    Voice and crisis.

    Bibliography: p.
    Includes index.
    1. Milton, John, 1608—1674—Criticism and interpreta-
tion.   2. Invocation in literature.   3. Inspiration in
literature.   4. Creation (Literary, artistic, etc.)
5. Prayer in literature.   I. Title.
PR3592.I58S35   1984   821'.4   84—2897
ISBN 0—208—02046—2 (alk. paper)

To GEORGE LORD AND MAYNARD MACK

Alas, 'tis true I have gone here and there
And made myself a motley to the view . . .

Contents

Preface

(This book aims to discover and interpret evidence of a fundamental
unity in Milton's poetry: a pattern of invocation, of the poet's calling
upon a source of inspiration. What I hope to show is, first, that the
very act of invocation is more pervasive in Milton than has been
realized previously; second, that this pervasive occurrence, together
with related themes and images, may have a significant pattern; and
third, that this pattern may provide a new vantage point for the
interpretation of Milton's poetry. To those who may remember Milton
only as a stern classicist or dogmatic Puritan, I hope to reveal the poet's
ardent, searching voice rising against all odds out of the blindness, the
conflicts, and the deadlocked silence of his fallen world toward the
isolated affirmation of a difficult, but inspiring, truth.

For these purposes, I explore the entire body of Milton's major
poetry: the lyric poems from "On the Morning of Christ's Nativity" to
"Lycidas," the *Mask*, *Paradise Lost*, *Paradise Regained*, and *Samson
Agonistes*. And I include some of the minor poems, notably "Ad
Patrem" and "Elegia Sexta" and Milton's translations of the Old
Testament Psalms. I also turn, where relevant, to the prose: particu-
larly "The Reason of Church Government," the *Second Defence*, the
preface to *Samson*.

In the introductory chapter, I attempt to set the stage by reviewing
the various uses and conceptions of invocation both within and outside
literature, emphasizing the religious dimension of invocation because
of its importance to Milton. In the second chapter, I organize the lyric
poetry and the *Mask* according to themes, images, and types of
invocation that reappear throughout Milton's poetry. I then examine
the four crowning examples of invocation in *Paradise Lost*, both to
identify their integral relationships to the epic structure and to explore
the poet's modulations of voice to celebrate, implore, understand, and

defend the mysterious source of his inspiration, as he confronts the possible triumphs and defeats of inspiration in a fallen world. In the last chapter, I study Milton's close relation as a poet to the Psalms in order to understand better the spiritual precedent for Milton's searching use of invocation throughout his poetry and, in particular, his use of invocation to apprehend a numinous Muse or to seek divine aid in times of crisis. In this context, the Psalms provide a basis both for reexamining the invocations of *Paradise Lost* and for understanding the importance of *Paradise Regained* and *Samson Agonistes* to the enduring pattern of voice and crisis in his poetry.

Quotations of Milton's poetry follow, in general, the Columbia edition, *The Works of John Milton;* quotations of his prose, the Yale edition, *Complete Prose Works of John Milton*. Occasional departures from the Columbia edition are made in order to obtain a translation I prefer. In Chapter 2, for example, I use the Carey edition, *The Poems of John Milton,* for the translation of "Ad Patrem," line 115, and the Hughes edition, *John Milton: Complete Poems and Major Prose,* for the other translations of Milton's Latin verse. These four modern editions, together with Thomas Newton's variorum edition of *Paradise Lost* (London, 1749), are the ones whose notes I have consulted most often.

While we hold some authors in a constant regard over a long period of time, others seem to lie in wait, catching us once and changing the face of the world. Such was Milton's hold upon me from almost the first day of my graduate studies at Yale University in the Milton seminar of Professor George deF. Lord, whose insights into the invocations of *Paradise Lost* prompted these explorations. Professor Maynard Mack, who directed the dissertation that became this book, like Raphael trying to educate Adam, descended from things of higher moment to help a friend compose his thoughts.

1 Introduction
The Dimensions of Invocation

Ye Muses, then, whoever ye are, . . .
Tom Jones

Invocation, like many forms of human expression, can be made to serve an extensive range of moods, from the sublime to the ridiculous, and, usually, our recognition of the ridiculous will depend on our memory of the sublime. Fielding's mock-epic appeal to the Muses in *Tom Jones* depends for its point on knowledge of a classical tradition that was already becoming in his time a province for the memory only, as his title for the chapter playfully asserts: "A battle sung by the muse in the Homerican style, and which none but the classical reader can taste." In the eighteenth century it was difficult to make a traditional epic invocation—indeed it proved impossible to write a serious epic at all. The most successful forms of invocation were devised by Pope for his mock-epic masterpieces *The Rape of the Lock* and *The Dunciad*. And, in the preceding century, Samuel Butler's *Hudibras* did not well prepare the reader, with its invocation to a jug of beer, for a presumptuous Puritan's invocation of a heavenly Muse.

To recall mock-epic is to remind ourselves that our notion of invocation need not—and should not—be confined to the serious, or, for that matter, to the epic. We remember that even ancient classical literature abounds in examples of invocation outside the epic mode. Whether in pastoral (Theocritus, Vergil), lyric (Pindar, Horace), or didactic (Hesiod, Lucretius) poetry, the poet can turn to the Muses for the inspiration to begin,

Sicilian Muses, let us sing now of somewhat higher things!
(Vergil, "Eclogue" IV)

1

to sustain,

> My Muse, steer the flight
> Of these my words . . .
>
> > (Pindar, "Nemea" 6)

or even to end his song:

> Run ahead and show me the way, as I
> run my race to the finish line, marked
> before me—thou, Calliope, nimble Muse.
>
> > (Lucretius, *De Rerum Natura* VI.92−94)[1]

The inspiring goddess may evoke a wide variety of attitudes, from Vergil's priest-like dedication in the *Georgics:* "May the sweet Muses whose holy emblems, under the spell of a mighty love, I bear, take me to themselves" (II.475−76), to Ovid's ironic distance in *The Art of Love:* "I will not falsely claim that my art is thy gift, O Phoebus, . . . neither did Clio and Clio's sisters appear to me while I kept flocks in thy vale, O Ascra: experience inspires this work: give ear to an experienced bard . . ." (I.25−29).[2] We also know that the Muses need not be the only object of a poet's call for aid. He may turn to another goddess, as Lucretius does at the beginning of *De Rerum Natura* when he invokes the aid of Venus. Or he may, like Tibullus, decide to invoke his absent friend instead.[3] In a more reverential strain, he may appeal to the ruling gods of the universe, as Pindar and Vergil sometimes do[4]—or as even Ovid does, when confronted by the vast challenge of the *Metamorphoses:*

> Of bodies chang'd to other shapes I sing.
> Assist, you Gods (from you these changes spring)
> And, from the Worlds first fabrick to these times,
> Deduce my never-discontinued Rymes.
>
> > (Sandys translation)[5]

The English tradition in poetry shows, as might be expected, a similar diversity. Chaucer's "invocacioun" to the god of sleep in *The House of Fame* insists on a special decorum appropriate to his subject: the god of sleep should be able to tell him about dreams. Spenser in "Epithalamion" chooses to rely on the tradition of the Muses, but adapts his portrait of them to the setting of his song: "Helpe me mine owne loues prayses to resound" (14). When, with the waning of the classical tradition, the English poet's formal traffic with the Muses declined, Blake could still sing poignantly in the traditional forms of invocation, even as he announced that it might never again be possible:

> Whether on Ida's shady brow,
>   Or in the chambers of the East,
> The chambers of the sun, that now
>   From antient melody have ceas'd;
>
> Whether in Heav'n ye wander fair,
>   Or the green corners of the earth,
> Or the blue regions of the air,
>   Where the melodious winds have birth;
>
> Whether on chrystal rocks ye rove,
>   Beneath the bosom of the sea
> Wand'ring in many a coral grove,
>   Fair Nine, forsaking Poetry!
>
> How have you left the ancient love
>   That bards of old enjoy'd in you!
> The languid strings do scarcely move!
> The sound is forc'd, the notes are few!
>
> ("To the Muses")

When the "Fair Nine" could no longer be found wandering through the landscape, the Romantics rediscovered the classical freedom of addressing other presences, including the landscape itself. Shelley created in his "Ode to the West Wind" a lyrical invocation of almost primitive force and excitement to a symbolic source of inspiration and renewal, culminating in a daring request to be united with it: "Be thou, Spirit fierce, / My spirit! Be thou me, impetuous one!" The odes of Keats are also, in substance, prolonged invocations to symbolic presences—a nightingale, a Grecian urn, a month, a season of the year, a goddess of late antiquity. As for Wordsworth, invocation becomes in him so characteristic an idiom that one critic has argued, "the landscape replaces the muse":[6]

> O sylvan Wye! thou wanderer thro' the woods,
> How often has my spirit turned to thee!
>
> "Tintern Abbey"
>
> And O, ye Fountains, Meadows, Hills, and Groves,
> Forebode not any severing of our loves!
>
> "Intimations Ode"

Nor need the invoked presences always be landscape. In one famous instance, the presence called on is that of the great invoker himself:

Milton! thou shouldst be living at this hour . . .

("London, 1802")

And when we reach modern times, such surrogates become the norm:

O sages standing in God's holy fire
As in the gold mosaic of a wall,
Come from the holy fire, perne in a gyre,
And be the singing-masters of my soul.

(Yeats, "Sailing to Byzantium")

Yeats, in his turn, becomes the sage that inspires Auden's famous elegy, with its charge to the "poet":

With your unconstraining voice
Still persuade us to rejoice . . .
In the prison of his days
Teach the free man how to praise.

While calling on the "Muse" by name has declined in modern poetic practice, it is difficult to believe that invocation itself can disappear as long as there is poetry, for invocation appears to express an inherent desire of the poet's voice:

even among these rocks
Sister, mother
And spirit of the river, spirit of the sea,
Suffer me not to be separated
And let my cry come unto Thee.

(Eliot, "Ash-Wednesday")

Hail, Muse! etc.
Don Juan

In essence, as we have seen, invocation is the poet's voice calling to a presence. Part of the hilarity in Byron's parody quoted above is the nonchalant use of "hail," a word that turns us back to the central instance in English poetry of invocation in the sublime style: "Hail, holy Light . . ." Another aspect of Byron's parody is his exclusion of the lyrical elaboration that makes Milton's invocation what it is, all dismissed with an *etc*. He gives us the two minimal requirements of invocation—the hailing and the Muse—but dismisses what matters most: the *voice* of the poet. Byron's *etc*. is, for Milton, the *sine qua non*.

For as the etymology of *invocation* suggests, the essential feature of the poet's *calling upon* a presence is his *vox*, his voice. This voice is at the very center of the phenomenon we know as invocation. Milton is only the most fully developed and self-conscious example of a voice-awareness that goes back to Homer. In ancient Greece, while the legendary founders of music were associated with various instruments, the Muses were celebrated for their entrancing voices: "unwearyingly flows the sweet sound from their lips."[7] The very name Calliope —Muse of epic poetry and mother of Orpheus, twice called "the Muse her self" in "Lycidas"—translates as "she of the beautiful voice."

Voice acquires its seventeenth-century potency, moreover, not only from Greek poetic tradition, but from Greek philosophy and the Bible. "Spoken words," begins Aristotle's treatise *On Interpretation*, "are the symbols of mental experience and written words are the symbols of spoken words."[8] Speech, therefore, has immediacy; writing has greater detachment and distance. Socrates makes the same point in the *Phaedrus*. There the king of Egypt is said to have rebuked the inventor of writing as follows: "this discovery of yours will create forgetfulness in the soul of learners, because they will not use their memories; they will trust to the external written characters and not remember of themselves. . . . [thus] you give your disciples not truth, but only the semblance of truth." With this verdict, Socrates agrees, adding: "writing is unfortunately like painting, for the creations of the painter have the attitude of life, and yet if you ask them a question they preserve a solemn silence."[9] For that matter, the very form of the Platonic dialogue depends on the illusion of voices encountering one another and the truth they share. Though involved in that spread of literacy that one scholar has described as the mark of Plato's generation in Greece,[10] the creator of the dialogues seems to make the fewest possible concessions to the "solemn silence" of the word not spoken; for "only in principles of justice and goodness and nobility taught and communicated orally for the sake of instruction and graven on the soul, which is the true way of writing, is there clearness and perfection and seriousness" (*Phaedrus*, 278).

The powers of speech idealized by Plato and Aristotle became institutionalized in the Roman world through such works as Cicero's *De Oratore* and Quintilian's *Institutio Oratoria*, and confirmed for

Christianity by the language of the Bible.[11] In Genesis, speech is the agent of Creation ("And God said . . .")—a theme that echoes through the entire canon: "In the beginning was the Word, and the Word was with God, and the Word was God." Biblical voice is a manifestation of presence, bridging the distance between Word and word. It is spoken on Sinai: "And the Lord spoke unto you out of the midst of the fire: ye heard the voice of the words, but saw no similitude; only *ye heard* a voice" (Deut. 4:12); it is acknowledged by Samuel in the temple: "Speak; for thy servant heareth" (1 Sam. 3:10); and it speaks out of the whirlwind to Job:

> Who is this that darkeneth counsel by words without
>   knowledge?
> Gird thee up now thy loins like a man; for I will demand of
>   thee, and answer thou me.
>
> (38:2−3)

In answering, the human voice pleads for access to the divine: "Let my prayer come before thee" (Psalm 88); cries out in the wilderness with the good news that a Messiah cometh; or cries out on the cross that the Great Voice has deserted it. In all this, for a poet of Milton's temper and religious commitment, there was an individual meaning waiting to be found, as we shall see.

Yeats's call to "the sages" to become his singing-masters and gather him "into the artifice of eternity" returns in spirit to the invocations of late antiquity. As Rome declined, the poet began to turn inward to his soul—as in the dying Emperor Hadrian's famous apostrophe. The Muses, too, underwent a strange transformation during this period, becoming identified as mysterious pagan goddesses able to aid in salvation and hence the subject of many inscriptions on sarcophagi.[12] At the same time, with the advent of Christianity and the early Church's critical rejection of the Muses, there became established among Christian poets a long tradition of anxiety about invoking a pagan Muse.[13]

This anxiety, of course, could not have persisted through the entire remaining life of the epic poem (well over a millenium after the Fall of Rome) unless the religious problem had been serious. And it was. For in its deepest historical roots, invocation is a religious, not a literary, phenomenon, appearing as the original form of divine worship in all cultures.[14]

The oldest surviving religious hymns and prayers illustrate this basic relation of man's voice to the mysteries that surround him. In the *Rigveda,* the most ancient of the Hindu canonical writings, most of the hymns are purely and simply invocations.[15] In ancient Greece, "all the (religious) hymns begin with invocations of the names of the gods to whom they are addressed. The invocation was believed to have an almost magic value."[16] The very appearance of the god indeed could depend "on the ritual that invokes him."[17] The emphasis on the efficacy of invocation was so great in Roman practice that "to know the right name of the competent deity was to possess a real power of compulsion over him."[18] For this very reason the names of the deities who guarded the safety of Rome were kept a state secret.

The ancient belief in the power of invocation was consistent enough to recognize its potential use to conjure devils and other evil powers by incantation. Today, we need go back no further than to Goethe or Marlowe to see that the vitality of the Faust legend depends on the continued consent of our imaginations to the darker powers of voice. To defend against those powers, the earliest religions often devised as an integral part of their invocations "spells and charms,"[19] so that the movement of the voice in prayer was simultaneously a dispelling of evil powers and a calling to beneficent ones—a dialectic of purification that recognized the mysterious affinity of the human voice with numinous powers of all kinds:

> But drive farr off the barbarous dissonance
> Of *Bacchus* and his revellers . . .
>
> (*Paradise Lost* VII.32−33)

Emphasis on the magical force of invocation is naturally strong among primitive religions.[20] The study of shamanism—a pervasive primitive form of religious mysticism, expressing itself in magical feats—not only indicates the primary importance of invocation in the shaman's ritual, but also provides a new perspective in which to view the functions of poetic invocation generally: "In preparing his trance, the shaman drums, summons his spirit helpers, speaks a 'secret language' or the 'animal language,' imitating the cries of beasts and especially the songs of birds. He ends by obtaining a 'second state' that provides the impetus for linguistic creation and the rhythms of lyric poetry."[21] In this ecstatic state, where his creation of poetry "remains an act of perfect spiritual freedom,"[22] the shaman-poet is also ready for

the exercise of seemingly magical powers, creating the illusion of
breaking the boundaries of space and time by a "magical flight" to the
sky, or a "visit to the underworld."[23] Thus his invocation, usually a
prolonged ritual of address to a multitude of divine and animal spirits,
is a necessary prelude both to his creation of poetry and to his attain-
ment of religious ecstasy and power. To achieve his "Ascent to the
Sky," for example, a shaman calls to "the Birds of Heaven": "Come to
me, singing!"[24] The birds possess the power, by their song, to lift him
to the imagined heights of his mystical journey. At the greatest
moment of his long "ascent," when his powers have reached their
summit, he stops to make an invocation to his god, "father Ulgan,
thrice exalted," praising him for creation ("Thou didst create all men,
Ulgan") and asking for the power to "withstand the Evil One." At the
moment of address to the Divine Father, "the culminating point of the
'ecstasy'," the shaman collapses, "exhausted."[25] He has used invocation both to prepare for his ecstasy and to crown it with his prayer.

It may well be, I think, that the great poet in civilized cultures
retains an important "primitive" function, retracing the radical unities
of man's aspirations.[26] Thomas Gray's portrait of Milton, for example,
like Wordsworth's well-known sonnet, endows him with powers that
would equally befit a shaman:

> Nor second He, that rode sublime
> Upon the seraph-wings of Extasy,
> The secrets of th' Abyss to spy.
> He pass'd the flaming bounds of Place and Time:
> The living Throne, the sapphire-blaze,
> Where Angels tremble, while they gaze,
> He saw . . .
>
> *(The Progress of Poesy)*

Perhaps a part of the authority we seem to grant the epic journeys
of Dante and Milton is based on their simulation of these "primitive"
capabilities: the visit to the underworld, the ascent to the sky. Certainly
each of these poets has earned a unique place in epic poetry and in
literature because of his inextricable combination of mysticism and
poetry; each draws strength from mystical sources outside the ordinary
literary tradition,[27] and each insists in the end upon the irreducible
transcendence of a personal journey, breaking the boundaries of space
and time. If the civilized poet (and no more civilized poet has ever
existed than Milton) can still discover "the world as though he were

present at the cosmogonic moment, contemporaneous with the first day of the creation," then we might say that "his attitude is strangely like that of the 'primitive,' of man in traditional society."[28] And if primitive man's invocation sometimes uses a secret animal language to express nostalgia for that unfallen world where man and beast could communicate in perfect freedom without fear,[29] his total act of prayer might be imagined not only to signify the human aspiration toward divine presence, but to foreshadow in an uncanny way the Miltonic nostalgia to experience the original human presence, a Paradise now lost.

Whether or not they appear to endow the ritual of invocation with magical or nostalgic significance, almost all cultures, primitive and civilized, seem to attest to the special power of the human voice when it rises in search of a divine response or in praise of an already felt presence. At such moments, man's voice becomes a self-renewing symbol of his deepest relation to the mysteries of his environment, seeming somehow to create the possibility it hopes for: to dwell, if only for a moment, within the hearing of a God.

In my distress I cried unto the Lord, and he heard me.
(Psalm 120)

For Western man, the Old Testament Psalms are among the most enduring forms of this experience. Characteristically opening with an invocation, these songs may then praise or confess, lament or rejoice, express confidence and hope or pray for deliverance from countless enemies; but each seems inherently to recognize the special value of man's unique gift for prayer and the unique power of his invocation: "Hear, O Lord, when I cry with my voice" (Psalm 27). Perhaps for this reason, the Psalms have always held a special position in the Jewish and Christian liturgies, both of which, to a degree we may not always be conscious of, depend on the act of invocation—in the collect and eucharistic prayer of Christian liturgy, for example, or in the Jewish Shema (hear) and recitation of the Psalms themselves.[30] Even the early Latin hymns of Christianity were modeled on the Old Testament lyrics; and most of them, such as Te Deum Laudamus, faithfully reflected the invocatory style of the Davidic songs.

A millenium later, the Protestant Reformation brought with it a spectacular revival of the Psalter, and during the sixteenth and seventeenth centuries the singing of the Psalms in the vernacular was a distinguishing feature of the Reformed faiths. Also during these two centuries, perhaps not accidentally, invocation became a synonym for prayer.[31] But "to call upon" *(invocare)* was to anticipate the possibility of being called: "be not silent to me" (Psalm 28), "Hear . . . and answer me" (Psalm 27). Invocation, in this sense, was a preparation for the many forms of divine response; and the most dramatic of these for Christians was the call of God: vocation. Augustine's *Confessions*, the first autobiography in the West, is a record of this dialectic between invocation and vocation. Its style—significantly—is based on the Psalms. Its content dramatizes the role of invocation in the total life of one man and his inner struggle to realize faith and direction. With it, for Christianity, invocation becomes the style of spiritual discovery. The Protestant Reformation was a reaffirmation of these Augustinian roots, reviving not only Augustine's immersion in the Psalms, but also his acute consciousness of the problem of vocation. Seventeenth-century Protestant poets, including Donne, Herbert, and Milton, show in their lives and writings a varied, but intense, experience of vocation.[32] Even a casual reader of Milton will remember the stress of vocation present in the famous sonnet "When I consider how my light is spent," with its anxiety that the "one Talent which is death to hide" has remained too hidden. Through the celebrated autobiographical passages of his prose writings, too, one becomes familiar with the pressures endured by a man who spent a lifetime learning and then realizing the demands of his unique calling, and whose motto of perfection was that a poet "ought him selfe to bee a true Poem."

Given such a spiritual disposition, does not the Augustinian precedent—the intimate intertwining of vocation and invocation—ask us to search for a similar dialectic in Milton? Indeed we would be surprised to find in a poet everywhere enthralled by his calling only one important instance of invocation, namely, those personal passages of *Paradise Lost* so justly famous since the publication of the epic. Yet where are the other instances? Are we not justified in searching for them in a poet who would have recognized the pervasiveness of invocation in the classical poetry that so often served as a model for his own? Would not such passages serve as a valuable guide to the consummation of the form in *Paradise Lost*? And might they not even provide new evidence of a fundamental unity in Milton's poetry? These are the questions I shall now try to address.

2 The Pattern of Invocation in Milton's Poetry

THE MIND THROUGH ALL HER POWERS

Of the great epic poets in Western literature, Milton seems most conscious of the imaginative possibilities inherent in the formulas of invocation and aspires most vigorously to realize them. Next to his invocations, those of Homer and Vergil appear simple, direct, and easy in their chains—in part, perhaps, because there is more they can take for granted in their audience's response:

> Sing in me, Muse, the man of many turns . . .
> *(The Odyssey)*

> Muse, remember the causes . . .
> *(The Aeneid)*

By contrast, Milton seems almost to have to create the image of the Muse he invokes.[1] It is not only that he has the perennial Christian concern about the use of a pagan custom; Tasso had the same concern with opposite results: lyrical creation gives way to theological homiletics in the opening of *Gierusalemme Liberata*. In Milton the historical challenge required—or at any rate produced—a quite new invention. His "Heavenly Muse" remains a Muse, but can respond to the deepest inclinations of mind and soul and not only the needs of epic memory. She is a development, rather than a rejection, of Homer's inspiring goddess, who "is heavenly, and is everywhere, and knows all things" (*Iliad* II). To the epic invocation he inherited, Milton added a dimension by calling in two features from outside the epic tradition: on the one hand, the religious forms of prayer and devotion; on the other, his own position as a lyric and epic poet.

No epic poet before Milton gave such lyrical elaboration to the formulas of invocation. Dante anticipated his dramatic use of the poet as participant in his own poem, but Dante's invocations are not sustained explorations of the poet's subjectivity. This is entirely appropriate to the *Divine Comedy* because the changing scenes themselves unfold in vivid and precise forms the inner landscape of the poet. The very subject of Dante's epic is his personal vision or, in a word, himself—however filtered by what he would have called a universal truth. Thus when Milton returns to the ancient classical models of epic and invocation, he pours into his invocations a version of the epic subjectivity that Dante had contributed to the tradition. The Dantesque tableau, the intense encounter, becomes in Milton the inward dialectic, the lyrical meditation in the presence of God; and Dante's use of invocation to mark the entrance into each of his three realms may lie behind Milton's strategy in placing his invocations at structurally important points.[2] The result is an extraordinary, and extraordinarily allusive, variation upon the classical procedures.

For Milton the epic invocation is a pattern of voicing through which the poet discovers—and asserts—his identity and his authority as an inspired singer:

> Sing Heav'nly Muse, that on the secret top
> Of *Oreb*, or of *Sinai*, didst inspire
> That Shepherd, who first taught the chosen Seed . . .
> (Paradise Lost I.6 – 8)

This pattern is something toward which the poet has been building since his very first exercise, his paraphrase of Psalm 114, and his ode, "On the Morning of Christ's Nativity," which is in some sense his record of his own birth as a poet. Milton prepares, whether consciously or by serendipity, for his culminating acts of epic invocation by a relentless earlier trying on of the possibilities of voice.

PRESENT TO THE INFANT GOD

Every reader recognizes that the first four stanzas of Milton's first major poem, "On the Morning of Christ's Nativity," are meant to serve as a formal introduction to the main body of the poem, "The Hymn." In fact, they are modeled on the Virgilian epic exordium—in which the first half introduces the subject, the second offers an explicit invocation. Stanzas 1 and 2 set forth time, subject, action:

1

This is the Month, and this the happy morn
Wherein the Son of Heav'ns eternal King,
Of wedded Maid, and Virgin Mother born,
Our great Redemption from above did bring;
For so the holy Sages once did sing,
    That he our deadly forfeit should release,
And with his Father work us a perpetual peace.

2

That glorious Form, that light unsufferable,
And that far-beaming blaze of Majesty,
Wherewith he wont at Heav'ns high Councel-Table,
To sit the midst of Trinal Unity,
He laid aside; and here with us to be,
    Forsook the Courts of everlasting Day,
And chose with us a darksom House of mortal Clay.

Just as clearly, the next two stanzas constitute the invocation
proper:

3

Say Heav'nly Muse, shall not thy sacred vein
Afford a Present to the Infant God?
Hast thou no verse, no hymn, or solemn strein,
To welcome him to this his new abode,
Now while the Heav'n by the Suns team untrod,
    Hath took no print of the approaching light,
And all the spangled host keep watch in squadrons bright?

4

See how from far upon the Eastern rode
The Star-led Wisards haste with odours sweet:
O run, prevent them with thy humble ode,
And lay it lowly at his blessed feet;
Have thou the honour first, thy Lord to greet,
    And joyn thy voice unto the Angel Quire,
From out his secret Altar toucht with hallow'd fire.

The unifying motif of these two stanzas is the poet's address to the
"Heav'nly Muse," and the opening words, "Say Heav'nly Muse,"
exactly foreshadow the language of the opening invocation of *Paradise*

Lost and the subsequent charge to the Muse:

> Sing Heav'nly Muse . . .
>
> (I.6)
>
> Say first . . .
>
> (I.27)

Such is the radical continuity in Milton's expressive patterns of invocation.

To the extent that the ode is itself a foreshadowing of epic, its opening appeal may be regarded as Milton's first conception of epic invocation. Through its wide ranging across past and future (the Fall, the Incarnation, the Redemption), not only are "distant ages" drawn into the present celebration, but the poem "acquires, even in its brief compass, the encyclopedic character prescribed by Renaissance critics as a feature of epic poetry."[3] Thus, in a sense, Milton comes into his poetic maturity at the moment when his imagination confronts a potentially epic subject; and for aid in this attempt he invokes the "Heav'nly Muse" to whom he will again turn for aid in the composition of *Paradise Lost*.

In another important way, the lines to Milton's future poetic development are discernible here. The opening of the ode stands in an integral relation to "The Hymn," anticipating the closeness of the later invocations to the structure of his epic, where the poet who prays "What in me is dark / illumin, what is low raise and support" (I.22−23) seems already to see the "darkness visible" and ultimate depths the story soon will reveal. "The Hymn," in fact, is like a miniature phantasmagorical epic (one can easily imagine a Miltonic "brief epic," like *Paradise Regained,* on the subject of the Nativity) whose introductory verses ask the Muse to participate in its main action:

> Hast thou no verse, no hymn, or solemn strein,
> To welcome him to this his new abode . . .?
>
> (17−18)

Like the epic poet's prayer, this invocation seeks to draw the story into the imagination's present—"See how from far upon the Eastern rode / The Star-led Wisards haste with odours sweet" (lines 22−23)—almost as if to make the true place of the action the poet's mind. This aspiration toward presence appears to give an early indication of the main temporal movement of "The Hymn," which begins in a past mode ("It *was* the winter wilde" [line 29]), but works to achieve a present tense—a labor secured in emphatically temporal terms in the pivotal eighteenth stanza:

> And then at last our bliss
> Full and perfet is,
>   But now begins . . .

$$(165-67)$$

With these lines, a new confidence carries the poem forward to its conclusion. "All the spangled host . . .in squadrons bright" (line 21) and "the Angel Quire" (27) of the invocation are at the poem's end descended to "the Courtly Stable" on earth, where "Bright-harnest Angels sit in order servicable" (243−44)—a descent from heaven that may anticipate the famous descents of heavenly spirits in *Paradise Lost:* of Raphael, within the epic action; and of the poet's Muse Urania.

Like Urania, the poet's first Muse must be endowed with "Voice divine" (*Paradise Lost* VII.2); in the ode's third stanza he implores her, "And joyn thy voice unto the Angel Quire." Milton's consciousness of the powers of voice makes its first appearance here. That Milton discovers his own voice as a poet while celebrating the "Infant God" is the underlying paradox of the third stanza and the poem, since the root meaning of "infant" is "one unable to speak." The Infant God is "the Word, unable to speak a word, swaddled in darkness," as Andrewes phrased it. And the poet's true "Present to the Infant God" is his own awakening voice. In "The Hymn," the Infant proclaims his arrival as the Word by conquering the voices of the old order, while the newly born poet acquires voice by celebrating the great event in prophetic strains. Just as *Paradise Lost* orients its first invocation toward the majestic figure of Moses, "That Shepherd, who first taught the chosen Seed," the ode looks toward the prophet Isaiah.[4] Milton reminds us in the first stanza of "the holy Sages" (the Hebrew prophets) who "once did sing" of the Messiah's coming, and in the last lines of the fourth stanza of the moment when the seraph takes the burning coal from the altar and places it on Isaiah's lips:

> And joyn thy voice unto the Angel Quire,
> From out his secret Altar toucht with hallow'd fire.

"Also," says Isaiah:

> I heard the voice of the Lord, saying
> Whom shall I send, and who will go for us?
> Then said I, Here am I; send me—
>
> (Isa. 6:8)

and almost as if in answer to the same question, Milton answers "O run, prevent them with thy humble ode," concluding his invocation with the very image of Isaiah's call.

If we allow ourselves to suppose that the composition of the Nativity Ode expresses either covertly or openly Milton's sense of his call to poetry, the echo of Isaiah is especially appropriate. The sense of vocation arises naturally, it would seem, from the invocation, almost as if the two ideas were interfused in Milton's mind, who cannot have been unaware of their common etymological root in "voice". We might even venture that his various *invocations*, culminating in those of *Paradise Lost*, are the steps by which he ascends to the fulfillment of *vocation*. The very images of the Nativity Ode stanzas anticipate the images to come. In the ode, it is from the Lord's "secret Altar" that the hallowed fire emerges. In *Paradise Lost*, it is from "the secret top" of Sinai that the Muse inspires. In both instances Milton remembers the radical Latin sense of *secretus* as "set apart," and uses the word to suggest the "separateness," the otherness, the transcendence of both experiences, and of the private vatic consciousness in which such experiences occur. The inspiration found in meditating on these scenes in Isaiah and Exodus comes to him in the "secret" place of his own characteristic vision, embodied finally in his blindness.

The First Light

Milton is preoccupied in the invocations of his ode and epic with *firstness*. In the epic's opening lines, he seeks the original inspiration and authority of that "first" (line 8) teacher of the chosen seed, and the spirit to whom he prays has been present "from the first" (line 19). In the ode he makes a similar plea:

> O run, *prevent* them . . .
>
> (24)

> Have thou the honour *first* . . .
>
> (26)

The plea is to arrive first, since to be a true prophet is *to speak before*.

Thus the Muse, in addition to serving as the source of his inspiration, must act as double for the eager poet, serving him as ambassador to the Nativity scene.

> O run, prevent them with thy humble ode
> And lay it lowly at his blessed feet

is a directive applicable to both functions, while the qualifying "humble" and "lowly" run counter to a deep undercurrent of poetic aspiration:

> Have thou the honour first, thy Lord to greet.

Here Milton seems to pose already the characteristic dilemma of his maturity—poetic ambition and Christian humility locked within one consciousness. He must "soar / Above th' *Aonian* Mount," yet "lay it lowly at his blessed feet."

The ode's invocational stanzas seem literally prophetic of the imagery and themes of the grand opening of *Paradise Lost*. This striking similarity is all the more interesting, since one is the first major example of his use of the invocatory mode and the other is one of the last examples, perhaps the very last, to be composed. Was there a kind of return, then, to poetic origins when Milton composed the invocations to *Paradise Lost*? It has always been clear that he regarded the Nativity Ode as occupying the first place in his poetic canon, and he always printed it first in his collected poems. Even in his account of the origins of the ode, in the December 1629 letter to Diodati, he emphasized that the *first* light of the Christmas dawn brought him the poem:

> Dona quidem dedimus Christi natalibus illa;
> Illa sub auroram lux mihi prima tulit.
>
> ("Elegia Sexta," 87−88)

> These are my gifts for the birth day of Christ—gifts which
>   the first light of its dawn brought to me.

Whether this account is literally true, and it may very well be, the manner in which he records it and his decision to emphasize the "first light" of dawn show something of the value he placed on temporal priority. Particularly expressive in this regard is the Latin construction *lux mihi prima*. The first light surrounds the poet *(mihi)*, and the poet is illuminated by it grammatically and poetically. The poetic self *(mihi)* even comes *before* the adjective "first" *(prima)*, and by its proximity to *prima* shares in the firstness of the light. In this sense, both *lux* and *mihi*, light and self, are *prima*. *Lux mihi prima,* one is tempted to say, sums up as in an emblem the situation of the poet in the great invocation to light in *Paradise Lost,* where the blind *mihi* is indeed surrounded by the *lux prima* and fervently prays that he may inwardly share that light, "ofspring of Heav'n *first-born*." In any case, we can recognize in the Christmas dawn described to Diodati "the approaching light" of the ode's own invocation, where time seems for a moment suspended in the now of the first light:

> Now while the Heav'n by the Suns team untrod,
>   Hath took no print of the approaching light.

ORPHEUS

While light is typically symbolic of divine transcendence in Milton's poetry, voice can represent the human and the divine and even the demonic. For the poet, voice implies a uniquely human capacity to encompass error as well as aspiration. Thus even while acquiring a triumphant voice in "The Hymn," he remembers the defeated voices of the ancient powers:

> The Oracles are dum,
>   No voice or hideous humm . . .
>
>   (173—74)
>
> A voice of weeping heard, and loud lament . . .
>
>   (183)
>
> The Nimphs in twilight shade of tangled thickets mourn · · ·
>   (188)
>
> The *Lars,* and *Lemures* moan with midnight plaint . . .
>   (191)

All these images are concentrated in just three stanzas (19—21), where also are heard a "hollow shriek," a "breathed spell," a "resounding shore," a "sighing," and "A drear and dying sound." These form a powerful elegaic contrast to the ideal union of voice and music represented earlier in the "holy Song" (line 133) that enraptures the "Shepherds on the Lawn" (line 85). To these pastoral poets, the arrival of "the mighty Pan" is heard as a

Divinely-warbl'd voice
Answering the stringed noise,
　　As all their souls in blissfull rapture took.

(96−98)

The significance of this ideal union of voice and music is best explained by Milton himself, in his Latin address to his father:

> When we return to our native Olympus and the everlasting ages of immutable eternity are established, we shall walk, crowned with gold, through the temples of the skies and with the harp's soft accompaniment we shall sing sweet songs to which the stars shall echo and the vault of heaven from pole to pole. Even now the fiery spirit who flies through the swift spheres is singing his immortal melody and unutterable song in harmony with the starry choruses. . . . And now, to sum it all up, what pleasure is there in the inane modulation of the voice without words and meaning and rhythmic eloquence? Such music is good enough for the forest choirs, but not for Orpheus, who by his song—not by his cithara—restrained rivers and gave ears to the oaks, and by his singing stirred the ghosts of the dead to tears. That fame he owes to his song.
>
> ("Ad Patrem," 30−37; 50−55)

This is Milton's most explicit defense of the mysterious and transcendent powers of the poetic voice. By emphasizing the song to the exclusion of the cithara, he insists on its priority, and this priority is essential to understanding the recurring appearance of the Orpheus myth in Milton's poetry: Orpheus *"by his song—not by his cithara—*restrained rivers and gave ears to the oaks, and *by his singing* stirred the ghosts of the dead to tears. That fame he owes to his *song."* The belief in poetic voice as the potential instrument of transcendent power could not be stronger. At the same time, as his later allusions show, Milton was never unaware of the tragic fate that can overtake the user of such power. The victory and the cost become inseparable in his mind.

In "Ad Patrem" itself, Milton attempts to show his father something of the powers of voice through the poem's opening lines:

Nunc mea Pierios cupiam per pectora fontes
Irriguas torquere vias, totumque per ora
Volvere laxatum gemino de vertice rivum;
Ut, tenues oblita sonos, audacibus alis
Surgat in officium venerandi Musa parentis.
Hoc utcunque tibi gratum, pater optime, carmen
Exiguum meditatur opus . . .

(1—7)

Now I wish that the Pierian fountains would send their
waters flooding through my breast and make my lips the
channel for the whole stream that pours from the twin
peaks, so that my Muse—her trivial songs forgotten—
might rise on bold wings to do honor to my revered father.
The song that she is meditating is a poor attempt, dearest
father, and not at all certain to please you . . .

The very phrase *audacibus alis* (on bold wings) discovers a mind already
intent on the audacious flight depicted in the invocations to *Paradise
Lost:* "Thee I revisit now *with bolder wing*" (III.13).

In the first seven lines of "Ad Patrem," Milton combines an
indirect invocation (stated tactfully as the object of the subjunctive verb
cupiam) of the Muse (lines 1—5) with a direct address to his father,
pater optime (6—7), revealing in this duality the true subject of the
poem; it is a contest between the Muse and his father. The directness of
the address to the father and the muffling of the appeal to the Muse
diplomatically place the father in the place of honor. Moreover, the
purpose of the appeal to the Muse is said to be only "to do honor to my
revered father" *(in officium venerandi . . . parentis)*. Significantly,
on the other hand, the only word separating *venerandi* from *parentis* in
the line is *Musa,* and the poet reserves the last address of the poem not
for his father (who is addressed in the preceding stanza), but for his
"youthful songs":

Et vos, O nostri, iuvenilia carmina, lusus, . . .

(115)

And you, my youthful poems, my pastimes, . . .

The last two "invocations" of the poem thus execute a final turning
from the demands of the father to those of the Muse. To understand
what is happening here, one must pay attention to Milton's choice of

words. By calling his poems *carmina* he asserts a vital connection between them and the *songs* of Orpheus, the basis of his defense of poetry to his father. *Carmen* is the word he uses repeatedly to describe the ideal poetic voice: *carmine, non cithara* (by his song—not by his cithara); and *habet has a carmine laudes* (that fame he owes to his song). Similarly, in the earlier section of "Ad Patrem," where the poet imagines the ideal union of voice and music in eternity, the word is *carmen: Dulcia . . . carmina* (sweet songs); and *inenarrabile carmen* (unutterable song). Hence, Milton's final application of this term to his own *carmina* evokes Orphean song to justify his vocational choice. The integrity of his defense demands, of course, that the claims of father and Muse be reconciled. On this account, even when the last stanza has made his choice clear, the young man vows that his Muse will preserve "the name of the father whom my song honors as an example to remote ages." The poem thus ends on the theme of reconciliation, visibly and gracefully advanced by the diplomacy of Milton's verse.

THE SON OF MEMORY

As in the appeal to his "youthful songs," the pattern of invocation in Milton's poetry may include, in its widest applications, the poet's relation to any source or symbol of inspiration or influence. Such is the case with his youthful poem "On *Shakespear*."[5] In this poem, published in the Second Folio of Shakespeare's plays (1632), he addresses a great predecessor in a way wholly characteristic:

> Dear son of memory, great heir of Fame,
> What need'st thou such weak witness of thy name?
>
> (5—6)

If we recall that the Muses are the daughters of Memory and Zeus, Milton's "Dear son of memory" can have the effect of making Shakespeare a male Muse, brother to the Nine, and therefore of establishing the entire poem as an invocation to him.[6] Just possibly he even plays on Shakespeare's words to his beloved in the sonnets:

> Be thou the tenth Muse, ten times more in worth
> Then those old nine which rimers invoke.
>
> (Sonnet 38)

Such, at any rate, is the degree of admiration in which Shakespeare is held by the aspiring poet. From our point of view, of course, there is an irony: after he declares his independence from his father, it is Milton himself who aspires to become a son of Memory. Invoked by later poets, he too will be "the great heir of Fame." The prayer of "Lycidas"—"So may some gentle Muse / With lucky words favor my destin'd Urn"—is an implied recognition of his own potential to be a Muse and to inspire future Muses. And the prayer eventually will be answered with such "lucky words" as these:

> Milton! thou shouldst be living at this hour . . .
>
> ("London, 1802")

Wordsworth knows this son of Memory lives; the invocation's magic brings him into life.

THE MARRIAGE OF VOICE AND VERSE

A similar extension of the invocational pattern occurs in "At a Solemn Musick":

> Blest pair of *Sirens,* pledges of Heav'ns joy,
> Sphear-born harmonious Sisters, Voice, and Vers,
> Wed your divine sounds, and mixt power employ
> Dead things with inbreath'd sense able to pierce . . .
>
> (1—4)

"The 'harmonious Sisters' are invoked as if they were Muses"[7] and celebrated for that collaboration that Milton had made the ideal of poetic song in "Ad Patrem." Moreover, the young poet's description of their "mixt power"—"Dead things with inbreath'd sense able to pierce"—seems to contain a clear allusion to the Orphean power that "stirred the ghosts of the dead to tears" ("Ad Patrem"). Where he had need to urge the necessary participation of the human voice in his defense before his father, he is now free to extol the combined powers of voice and music heard in the eternal heaven of "Ad Patrem" ("with the harp's soft accompaniment we shall sing sweet songs") and here represented in a similar setting:

> And to our high-rais'd phantasie present
> That undisturbed Song of pure concent,
> Ay sung before the saphire-colour'd throne
> To him that sits thereon

With Saintly shout, and solemn Jubily,
Where the bright Seraphim in burning row
Their loud up-lifted Angel trumpets blow,
And the Cherubick host in thousand quires
Touch their immortal Harps of golden wires,
With those just Spirits that wear victorious Palms,
Hymns devout and holy Psalms
Singing everlastingly . . .

(5–16)

The poem may itself be described as a celebration of the marriage of Voice and Verse: "*Wed* your divine sounds."[8] The poet seems to find their harmony an echo of the celestial turning of the spheres, for he calls them the "Sphear-born harmonious Sisters." Perhaps he remembers that verse itself is a form of turning (Latin *vertere*, "to turn"). Appropriately, at the very center of the poem is a turning that shifts the focus from heavenly example to earthly imitation—another version, perhaps, of the descent from heaven. For in heaven the angels are

Singing everlastingly;
That we on Earth with undiscording voice
May rightly answer that melodious noise . . .

(16–18)

It is the "undiscording *voice*" of man that must rise to the transcendent occasion. Milton's choice of the "holy Psalms" (line 15) to identify ideal song is particularly interesting, because the Psalms themselves are based on an invocation pattern, and his ideal of singing to the harp's accompaniment is a description of their essential nature (the Greek root *psalmos* translates as "songs sung to the harp"). Furthermore, the invocation to Verse makes it possible to read this poem on one level as Milton's own attempt to "rightly answer" the "holy Psalms," if we remember that the English biblical meaning of "verse" (as in "chapter and verse") originated from its application to "one of the sections of a psalm or canticle corresponding to the compound unit (usu. a couplet) of Hebrew poetry" *(Oxford English Dictionary)*. It seems possible, therefore, that, by invoking Verse as one of his twin Muses, he intends to affirm his aspiration to be a psalmist poet, and hence sets out to create in his invocation a personal interpretation of what should "rightly answer" the inspired Psalms. Their appearance in this invocation-lyric is thus possibly a revealing one, signaling a psalmist background to Milton's total sense of what the experience of invocation should be in its most transcendent phase. The "inbreath'd sense" (line 4) for which the poet prays is the inspiration to pierce "dead things," including the dead words to which the poet magically, Orpheus-like, gives life. In this way, the figures of Orpheus and the psalmist are associated, and their common symbol—the "Harp and Voice"—will haunt Milton's imagination through the years.

The subject of "At a Solemn Musick" is ultimately the same as that of *Paradise Lost*. For

> disproportion'd sin
> Jarr'd against natures chime, and with harsh din
> Broke the fair musick that all creatures made
> To their great Lord, whose love their motion sway'd
> In perfect Diapason, whilst they stood
> In first obedience, and their state of good.
>
> (19–24)

The diction of the last clause seems particularly to look forward to the rhetoric of *Paradise Lost:* "Sufficient to have stood, though free to fall." It is the Fall that measures the distance between Milton's own "psalm" and the "holy Psalms" he can just begin to hear in his imagination. And the prayer with which this invocation ends is the central hope expressed in the opening lines of *Paradise Lost*, the hope of paradise regained—to "regain the blissful seat":

> O may we soon again renew that Song,
> And keep in tune with Heav'n, till God ere long
> To his celestial consort us unite,
> To live with him, and sing in endless morn of light.
>
> (25–28)

The image of redemption as a renewed song is consistent with the young poet's high expectations of his vocation as a singer. "Milton seems almost to be consecrating his life and art to a purpose figured forth as a liturgical one."[9]

Moving from past to future, from Fall to Redemption, the triumphant resolution represents the poem's final "turning," almost as if the passage were the epode of a Greek choral ode. The poet's insistence on "we" throughout his lyric only makes this possibility seem more suggestive, implying that "we on Earth" constitute a kind of chorus whose heavenly model is "the Cherubick host in thousand quires." More specifically, the structure seems to correspond precisely with the Greek ode's pattern of strophe (lines 1−16), antistrophe (17−24), and epode (25−28)—moving from heaven's high chorus to earth's fallen one and, finally, to our hoped-for participation in the "celestial consort." If this is the case, the turning that we saw imaged in the harmony of the spheres and even of Verse itself is embodied in the poem's very structure. Such a perfect fusion of Greek and Hebrew sources—of ode and psalm—should be no surprise to readers long accustomed to Milton's epic welding of Homer and Genesis. If this lyric can be said to "renew" those ancient forms, its focus on "Song" at the close is all the more allusive, recalling those antecedents as it crowns the ideal marriage that resonates in Milton's other poems.

POETA LUDENS

"L'Allegro" and "Il Penseroso" present charmingly the picture of a poet "married to immortal verse," but not yet hooked on a particular Muse. This new version of vocational choice—what kind of singer to be—is represented as a contest between two Muses, each of whom is explicitly called on to appear with all her retinue of attractions:

> But com thou Goddess fair and free,
> In Heav'n ycleap'd *Euphrosyne*,
> And by men, heart-easing Mirth . . .
> ("L'Allegro," 11−13)

> But hail thou Goddess, sage and holy,
> Hail divinest Melancholy . . .
> ("Il Penseroso," 11−12)

The happy man invoking "heart-easing Mirth" is not the only playful spirit evidenced by these poems. Despite their often-noted resemblance to academic exercises, the air of spontaneity that breathes in them arises as if from the spirited performance of a musical invention. Instead of the classical motif of the disastrous challenge by a bold poet to the Muses (a motif that later grips the audacious poet of *Paradise Lost*), the young man here shrewdly devises a contest between two goddesses to decide which he will choose as his Muse. Neither is one of the traditional Nine, and to that extent her image as a Muse has to be created:

> But com thou Goddess fair and free,
> In Heav'n ycleap'd *Euphrosyne,*
> And by men, heart-easing Mirth,
> Whom lovely *Venus* at a birth
> With two sister Graces more
> To Ivy-crowned *Bacchus* bore;
> Or whether (as som Sager sing)
> The frolick Wind that breathes the Spring,
> *Zephir* with *Aurora* playing,
> As he met her once a Maying,
> There on Beds of Violets blue,
> And fresh-blown Roses washt in dew,
> Fill'd her with thee a daughter fair,
> So bucksom, blith, and debonair.
>
> ("L'Allegro," 11−24)

At the outset, posing the question of heaven's vs. earth's name for the Muse seems innocent enough. But the question of what constitutes the Muse's right name is later deeply embedded in Milton's embattled call to Urania in *Paradise Lost:*

> Descend from Heav'n *Urania,* by that name
> If rightly thou art called . . .
>
> (VII.1−2)

Perhaps the question is rooted at the deepest level in the ancient belief that invoking a divine power by its correct name gives one a kind of magical power over it, allowing one to compel its presence and enlist its aid. Whether or not this is so, it is apparent that the naming of the Muse is problematic in the lyric and in the epic, leading the poet to account for her background and identity. In both passages, the section on naming is immediately reinforced by the fiction of the Muse's origins. "L'Allegro," in a characteristically sportive mood, entertains alternate possibilities with quick sleight of hand: "Or whether (as som Sager sing)." Venus and Bacchus, or Zephir and Aurora—either set of parents will do. The later Milton guides the development of the fiction into consonance with the theme of the epic about to be explored, Creation:

> . . . for thou
> Nor of the Muses nine, nor on the top
> Of old *Olympus* dwell'st, but Heav'nlie borne,
> Before the Hills appeerd, or Fountain flow'd,
> Thou with Eternal wisdom didst converse,
> Wisdom thy Sister, and with her didst play
> In presence of th' Almightie Father, pleas'd
> With thy Celestial Song.
>
> (VII. 5 – 12)

Interestingly enough, in view of the great differences, the common theme of creative play dominates both this account and the one in "L'Allegro": "*Zephir* with *Aurora* playing, / As he met her once a Maying, . . . Fill'd her with thee a daughter fair." The creative play depicted by the poet in both cases provides a kind of divine sanction for his own play in creating the fiction of the Muse and, ultimately, the poem itself.

Even Melancholy, the Muse of "Il Penseroso," must be given an appropriate birth by the fertile mind of the poet, a "higher" birth that nonetheless results from the sexual divagations of the gods:

> Thee bright-hair'd *Vesta* long of yore,
> To solitary *Saturn* bore;
> His daughter she (in *Saturns* raign,
> Such mixture was not held a stain)
> Oft in glimmering Bowres and glades
> He met her, and in secret shades
> Of woody *Ida's* inmost grove,
> While yet there was no fear of Jove.
>
> (16 – 30)

In comparison with the parallel passage in "L'Allegro," the logic here is more contorted, just as the genealogy is more bizarre: Melancholy is the result of an incestuous relationship between a virgin and her solitary father. Here one feels that the young recluse speaking has made a slightly clumsy attempt to capture the mystical aura of the Christian paradox expressed in St. Bernard's famous prayer in the *Paradiso:* "*Vergine madre, figlia del tuo figlio*" (Virgin mother, daughter of thy son). In any case, the Pensive One settles upon a single fiction, compared with the choice offered in "L'Allegro"; and the themes of chasteness and solitude embedded in that fiction are fundamental to the life envisioned by "Il Penseroso".

The final effect of the choice between these visions is imagined to be living with the Muse, not just singing with her:

> These delights, if thou canst give,
> Mirth with thee, I mean to live.
>
> ("L'Allegro," 151 – 52)

> These pleasures *Melancholy* give,
> And I with thee will choose to live.
>
> ("Il Penseroso," 175 – 76)

Echoing Marlowe's famous proposition to his beloved, the end of each poem treats the Muse as a potential mistress, who will provide "delights" or "pleasures" appropriate to her nature. The eager poet looks forward to a future of active participation with these Muses in the creative playfulness that begot them in the first place, and the result will be his poems.[10] Perhaps he can even find a way not to miss the opportunity of living with each one. Such a strategy certainly would be in the spirit of the gods. But living (as opposed to singing) with a Muse is also a way of symbolizing commitment. From beginning to end, each poem is an invocation intent on imagining the vocational results of choosing a particular source of inspiration. The natural evolution of the poems' scenes out of the character of the Muse each invokes makes it clear that the pressure of choice is inherent in the invoking moment and that every important invocation defines an approach to experience. But because the final choice eludes the structure and fiction of the twin poems, it can be prolonged beyond their horizon. For now, it is unnecessary and perhaps even too restrictive. "The hidden soul of harmony" seems, in its way, as alluring a discovery as "all Heav'n" brought before the eyes. Process is more important than progress here, as the power to imagine choices seems to be for the moment more crucial than the alternative chosen. Invocation becomes an open-ended experiment in identity.

BARBAROUS DISSONANCE

But to discover "the hidden soul of harmony," the "melting voice" of "L'Allegro" must run "through mazes"—presumably gliding by the dangers and pitfalls that lie therein. Likewise, the prelude to

"Il Penseroso's" vision is pacing "the studious Cloysters pale," a symbol of the enclosure and silence that must precede ecstasy and voice. Both the labyrinth and the cloister are present, of course, as benign obstacles; their very restrictions make transcendence possible. Yet their incorporation into the moment of triumph serves to remind us of the dialectical nature of Milton's imagination, reflected in the very form of the twin poems: a parallel structure of opposing voices.

Each poem begins by announcing a ritualistic casting out of obstacles to the transcendence of its own particular voice and vision. This movement occupies the first ten lines, followed in each case by the first line of invocation:

> Hence loathed Melancholy
>   Of *Cerberus*, and blackest midnight born,
> In *Stygian* Cave forlorn.
>   'Mongst horrid shapes, and shrieks, and sights unholy,
> Find out some uncouth cell,
>   Where brooding darkness spreads his jealous wings,
> And the night-Raven sings;
>   There under *Ebon* shades, and low-brow'd Rocks,
> As ragged as thy Locks,
>   In dark *Cimmerian* desert ever dwell.
> But com thou Goddess fair and free . . .
>   ("L'Allegro," 1—11)

> Hence vain deluding joyes,
>   The brood of folly without father bred,
> How little you bested,
>   Or fill the fixed mind with all your toyes;
> Dwell in som idle brain,
>   And fancies fond with gaudy shapes possess,
> As thick and numberless
>   As the gay motes that people the Sun Beams,
> Or likest hovering dreams
>   The fickle Pensioners of *Morpheus* train.
> But hail thou Goddess, sage and holy . . .
>   ("Il Penseroso," 1—11)

The reader's first tendency may be to think of these as celebrated, but isolated, instances of poetic apotropaism. The ritual recurs, however,

at decisive turns in Milton's later invocations. In "Lycidas," for
example, the apotropaic moment is fully integrated into the invocation:

> Begin then, Sisters of the sacred well,
> That from beneath the seat of *Jove* doth spring,
> Begin, and somewhat loudly sweep the string.
> *Hence with denial vain, and coy excuse* . . .
>
> (15 – 18)

The language even echoes the dismissal of "Il Penseroso": "*Hence vain
deluding joyes* . . ." And the echo spreads even further when, later in
"Lycidas," the poet contemplates the "vain deluding joyes" of
"*Amaryllis* in the shade" (line 68) and "the tangles of *Neaera's* hair"
(69) and asks, ironically, if poetry is not in fact the vainest of all
delusions:

> Alas! What boots it with uncessant care
> To tend the homely slighted Shepherds trade,
> And strictly meditate the thankless Muse,
> Were it not better don as others use,
> To sport with *Amaryllis* in the shade,
> Or with the tangles of *Neaera's* hair?
>
> (64 – 69)

In "L'Allegro" and "Il Penseroso" the apotropaic passages are isolated
and precede the forward motion of the invocation and the poem. In
"Lycidas" both movements constitute an intricate simultaneous turning of the poet. The entire poem is the dramatization of this turning,
and the success is secure only in the final line: "To morrow to fresh
Woods, and Pastures new."

These movements enable the poet to perform his necessary self-
correction and self-education:

> What in me is dark
> Illumin, what is low raise and support . . .
>
> (*Paradise Lost* I.22 – 23)

As in the "Lycidas" lines, the invocations of *Paradise Lost* turn away
obstacles to the triumph of poetic voice: "all mist from thence / Purge
and disperse" (III.53 – 54). Earlier, the same invocation told of
overcoming another obstacle—"Escap't the *Stygian* Pool"—just as the
speaker of "L'Allegro" had exiled Melancholy to "some uncouth

cell . . . In *Stygian* Cave forlorn." Whether pool or cave, the Stygian atmosphere seems one of despair and silence, where voice has failed. Thus the blind epic poet first escapes the Stygian threat to voice, then prays for the dispersal of the mist threatening the mind's vision. The plea of the voice for light depends upon the successful overcoming of both dangers.

The apotropaic aspect of the invocation pattern makes its final, most violent, appearance in the invocation of *Paradise Lost*, Book VII:

> But drive farr off the barbarous dissonance
> Of *Bacchus* and his revellers, the Race
> Of that wilde Rout that tore the *Thracian* Bard
> In *Rhodope,* where Woods and Rocks had Eares
> To rapture, till the savage clamor dround
> Both Harp and Voice; nor could the Muse defend
> Her Son.
>
> (VII.32−38)

Here the aspect of ritual seems to fade before the urgency of the threat, revealed in the poet's almost obsessive elaboration of the Orphic death theme, reaching its climax in the drowning of "Harp and Voice." The most violent and most poignant assertion of apotropaic energies is made when the danger confronted is a direct and urgent threat to "Voice" (line 37) and, therefore, to invocation itself. The poet's careful and deliberate stress on "*Both* Harp and Voice" we now recognize as the culmination of the theme earlier sounded in "Ad Patrem" and "At a Solemn Musick": the ideal union of voice and music that Milton had also identified with Orpheus in those early poems.

The figure of Orpheus appears in "L'Allegro" and "Il Penseroso" to be a counterpoint to the two approaches to experience. The appearance of Orpheus is in fact the climactic mythological representation of "L'Allegro," where the imagined effect of "untwisting all the chains that tie / The hidden soul of harmony" is

> That *Orpheus* self may heave his head
> From golden slumber on a bed
> Of heapt *Elysian* flowres, and hear
> Such streins as would have won the ear
> Of *Pluto,* to have quite set free
> His half regain'd *Eurydice.*
>
> (145−50)

While this contrary-to-myth subjunctive clause, depicting the resur-
rection of Orpheus in Elysium and his total liberation of Eurydice, is a
persuasive triumph of the poetic fancy of "L'Allegro," it is possibly one
of the "vain deluding joyes" exiled by "Il Penseroso." Indeed at this
point the song of innocence almost threatens to become a song of
experience. (One wonders about the possibility that "L'Allegro" and
"Il Penseroso" were an exemplary influence on Blake's conception of
Songs of Innocence and Experience.) Similarly, the song of experience
verges on innocence when "Il Penseroso" records the triumph, without
hinting of the tragedy, of Orpheus—forgetting that Eurydice was only
"half regain'd":

> Or bid the soul of Orpheus sing
> Such notes as warbled to the string,
> Drew Iron tears down *Pluto's* cheek,
> And made Hell grant what Love did seek.
>
> (105−8)

The agent of this liberation is "the soul" of the mythical bard singing to
his harp—in a sense, "the hidden soul of harmony" celebrated not by il
penseroso, but by l'allegro:

> Lap me in soft *Lydian* Aires
> Married to immortal verse,
> Such as the meeting soul may pierce
> In notes, with many a winding bout
> Of lincked sweetness long drawn out,
> With wanton heed, and giddy cunning,
> The melting voice through mazes running;
> Untwisting all the chains that tie
> The hidden soul of harmony.
>
> ("L'Allegro," 136−44)

The passage is the climax of "L'Allegro's" invocation to the Muse, and
the request is to marry music and voice, as in a different way it is the
climactic request of "Il Penseroso":

> There let the pealing Organ blow
> To the full voic'd Quire below,
> In Service high, and Anthems cleer,
> As may with sweetness, through mine ear,
> Dissolve me into extasies,

And bring all Heav'n before mine eyes.

                              ("Il Penseroso," 161—66)

The "melting voice" of "L'Allegro" and the "full voic'd Quire" of "Il Penseroso" are the culminating images of voice in these poems. Each is balanced with, and "married to," a corresponding image of music: "soft *Lydian* aires" and "the pealing Organ."[11] The first passage searches for deep inner harmony; the second, for mystical self-transcendence. Yet, in both these moments, the poems turn inward in search of their own deepest foundations as poems, and what each finds is in essence the sound of its own voice.

 ## SWEET ECHO

When Milton turned aside for a moment from his lyric poetry to create his *Mask* for presentation at Ludlow Castle, he seems to have found invocation so deeply embedded in his poetic consciousness that the *Mask* itself became a tribute to its powers. Its demonic capabilities are recognized when out of Comus's first speech emerge such words as these:

> Hail Goddess of Nocturnal sport,
> Dark vail'd *Cotytto*, t' whom the secret flame
> Of mid-night Torches burns; mysterious Dame,
> That ne're art call'd but when the Dragon woom
> Of Stygian darkness spets her thickest gloom,
> And makes one blot of all the air,
> Stay thy cloudy Ebon chair,
> Wherin thou rid'st with *Hecat'*, and befriend
> Us thy vow'd Priests . . .

                              (128—36)

The passage is a full-fledged demonic parody of the interrelation of vocation and invocation. Comus knows that he remains the "vow'd Priest" of the power he invokes. When the lady enters, her speech provides the invocatory counterpoint: "O welcom pure-ey'd Faith . . ." (lines 213—20). The powers of voice implicitly recognized in this prayer are then beautifully celebrated in the lady's famous song, invoking *"Sweet Echo, sweetest Nymph that liv'st unseen . . ."*[12] Comus rightly calls this "Divine inchanting ravishment" (line 244), recognizing

> Sure something holy lodges in that brest,
> And with these raptures moves the vocal air
> To testifie his hidd'n residence . . .
>
> (246—48)

Luxuriating in this "*vocal* air," he is moved to greet her—"Hail forren wonder"—almost as if her lovely voice were that of a Muse: "such a sacred, and home-felt delight, . . . I never heard till now" (lines 262—64). What Comus in his fascination discovers is the transcendent dimension of invocation, the "Divine inchanting ravishment" of the human voice in its plea for aid.

The dramatic situation of the masque also anticipates the poet's self-dramatization in the invocations of his epic. The attendant spirit's reliance on the authority of "the sage Poets taught by th' heav'nly Muse" (line 514) already discovers the very phrase with which the epic poet crystallizes his own authority: "Taught by the heav'nly Muse" (*Paradise Lost* III.19). Moreover, the endangered purity of the lady, ensnared in the dark wood by the son of Bacchus and "a rout of Monsters," is analogous to the embattled situation of the poet of "upright heart and pure" (I.18), threatened and besieged by the "wilde Rout" of "Bacchus and his revellers," "in darkness and with dangers compast round" (VII.34, 37, 23). The very same phrase—"barbarous dissonance"—describes the lady's enemies in the masque (line 549) and the epic poet's (VII.32).

The ideal of sexual purity is a major recurrent symbol in the early Milton of the preparation for, and dedication to, the life of a poet.[13] In "Lycidas," "To sport with *Amaryllis* in the shade" (line 68) and to "strictly meditate the thankless Muse" (66) are mutually *exclusive* preoccupations for the serious poet. It is not difficult to see how Milton's drama of "insnared chastity" *(Mask,* line 908) might become a proving ground for the poet's "insnared" vocation at a time when a successful masque was perhaps the best evidence the young man could offer his musician-father of his destined calling.

The world of the *Mask* is a maze of sound: "guided by mine ear I found the place," the spirit says. The lady's misfortune is to be lost for a time in such a maze:

> *Comus.* What chance good Lady hath bereft you thus?
> *Lady.* Dim darkness, and this leavie Labyrinth.
>
> (276—77)

The characters wander through this labyrinth as their voices search the darkness for light: "Eie me blest Providence . . ." (line 328) the lady prays, walking "In the blind mazes of this tangl'd Wood" (line 180) with the enemy her only guide, while her elder brother pleads with the powers he can *see:*

> Unmuffle ye faint Stars, and thou fair Moon
> That wontst to love the travellers benizon,
> Stoop thy pale visage through an amber cloud,
> And disinherit *Chaos,* that raigns here
> In double night of darkness and of shades;
> Or if your influence be quite damm'd up
> With black usurping mists, som gentle taper,
> Though a rush Candle from the wicker hole
> Of some clay habitation visit us
> With thy long levell'd rule of streaming light,
> And thou shalt be our star of Arcady,
> Or *Tyrian* Cynosure.   (330—41)

The lady's pathway out of the acoustical labyrinth is to come, however, not as light, but as song. She is saved by the great "Song" that constitutes the climax of the drama, so much so that the *Mask* itself may be regarded, in one commentator's phrase, as "the triumph of song."[14] The interesting thing from our point of view is that the song is cast in the form of a sustained invocation to Sabrina:

> Sabrina fair
>   Listen where thou art sitting
> Under the glassie, cool, translucent wave,
>   In twisted braids of Lillies knitting
> The loose train of thy amber-dropping hair,
>   Listen for dear honours sake,
>   Goddess of the silver lake,
>   Listen and save.
>   (859—866)

A second stanza of invocation builds upon the language of the song:

> Listen and appear to us . . .
> Till thou our summons answerd have.
>   Listen and save.
>   (867, 888—889)

The refrain of these stanzas beautifully summarizes the shared dimensions of invocation and prayer: *"Listen and save."* When, in response to this call, "Sabrina *rises, attended by water-Nymphs, & sings,"* her song evolves lyrically through a complex language of description, echoing the language and style of the invocation to her, but ending in the simple declaration, *"I am here"* (line 900). Thus the invocation gains the presence it seeks. If the appeal to Sabrina can be said to form the counterpoint to the earlier invocation to Echo, then the implied lesson seems to be that the sweetest echo is divine response. The transcendent dimension intuited by Comus listening to the Echo becomes fully manifest before the eyes of all in the great spectacle of Sabrina's appearance and song. Uniting vision and voice and music, Milton creates his most sustained and elaborate celebration of the primitive and seemingly magical powers of invocation.

"I am here" speaks for the poet, who finds himself once more out of the woods and on the path of the vocation he recognizes as his own.

THE DREAD VOICE IS PAST

In "Lycidas" the poet becomes "insnared" by the thought of mortality: "Bitter constraint, and sad occasion dear" (line 6) compel the song. The challenge to voice and life is nowhere more evident or more crucial. The pastoral mode of the poem is itself significant. For Milton (as for Pope after him), aware of the Vergilian progression of pastoral, georgic, and epic, the pastoral mode is the self-consciously initiatory phase of the serious poet's vocation.[15] It is, in a real sense, the test of vocation. The pastoral song of the "uncouth Swain" (line 186) becomes the rite of passage to Milton's epic ambition and the final turning of his youth in the labyrinth of poetic selfhood.

The invocations of "Lycidas" reflect the pressures, 'the "uncessant care" (line 64), of vocation. The "laborious dayes" (72) of which the "uncouth Swain" complains are laborious, at least partly, because they are preparing for a new birth. When this birth finally occurs, when this poem is born, it cries aloud under the shadow of death and in uncertain relation to the sometimes "thankless Muse" (line 66). "The relation of the poet to the Muse—even the question whether the Muse has any existence apart from the poet himself—is . . . crucial for the theme of the poem."[16] The elegy becomes Milton's chosen confrontation with the possible defeat of his own poetic self. The poem is a victory for the young Milton, but a victory with a cost and with new burdens and new responsibilities.

"Lycidas" is a polyphony of voices: invocations, apostrophes, and various modes of direct address are repeatedly sounded through the poem's charged atmosphere. In no other Miltonic poem is the atmosphere of hidden conflict so pervasive, and the variety and force of voice so evident. In this respect, its role may be analogous to that of *The Waste Land* in Eliot's development. Indeed Eliot's poem may be aptly described in the same words that G. Wilson Knight used to describe "Lycidas": "an accumulation of magnificent fragments."[17]

In "Lycidas" there is a multiple pattern of invocation, with at least six instances (three examples of double calling) and possibly more, depending on how the difficult distinction is made in this poem between invocation and apostrophe. For example, in the famous opening lines, Milton summons up the energies to begin, with an apostrophic appeal:

> Yet once more, O ye Laurels, and once more
> Ye Myrtles brown, with Ivy never sear,
> I com to pluck your Berries harsh and crude . . .

These lines are not merely an apostrophe; the reader rightly feels that they charge and recharge the opening energies of the poem as an invocation would. The mood is invocatory, even if one finally decides the mode is not. The laurels are felt as an inspirational presence and, in that sense, a Muse. As the symbol of fame, they represent "the spur that the clear spirit doth raise." Yet the approach to the Muse is rough: "I com to pluck your Berries harsh and crude." The repetition of *once more* signals that the poet *re*ascends, "though hard and rare." The opening lines provide an example of a voice pattern in "Lycidas" that should not be labeled "invocation"—and yet the reader misses something if he does not see the fundamental resemblance.

Similarly, in the transition to the final movement of the poem, there are tightly clustered in three lines three eruptions of apostrophic voice that seem to border on invocation:

> Look homeward Angel now, and melt with ruth.
> And, O ye *Dolphins*, waft the haples youth.
> Weep no more, woful Shepherds weep no more . . .
>   (163−65)

Each of the figures to which the poet calls is a transfigured presence: the "Angel" is the divine *genius loci* of St. Michael's Mount; the *"Dolphins"* are themselves mythical symbols of transfiguration (whichever of the proposed mythological contexts is accepted—the Arion myth or the story of Palaemon); and the "woful Shepherds" seem to be Milton's idealized image for surviving poets, which he substitutes, significantly, for the Muses who appear in Theocritus at a parallel moment in the structure of the farewell to Daphnis: "Cease, O Muses, cease your pastoral songs" ("Idyll" I). All three are transformed presences, and Milton invokes them in rapid succession to aid him in the most difficult and sublime transition of the poem, the transition to the transfiguration of Lycidas:

> In the blest Kingdoms meek of joy and love.
> There entertain him all the Saints above,
> In solemn troops, and sweet Societies
> That sing, and singing in their glory move,
> And wipe the tears for ever from his eyes.
>
> (177—81)

In that transition, apostrophe borders on invocation because of the transfiguration of those presences to which the poet calls, and this process anticipates the final transfiguration of the poem, the exaltation of Lycidas himself. The tension between apostrophe and invocation seems almost to be the characteristic atmosphere of "Lycidas," an atmosphere charged with the eruption of voice. And, in this central but utterly unique entry in the Miltonic canon, the continual eruption of voice is one indicator of the emblazoned atmosphere of tension. Invocation becomes the recurrent and crucial mode of transition, in a poem that often seems to be an accumulation of magnificent transitions.

The first invocation of the poem enters at line 15:

> Begin then, Sisters of the sacred well,
> That from beneath the seat of *Jove* doth spring,
> Begin, and somewhat loudly sweep the string . . .

Here we have a double "beginning," a double call to the Muses, who are invoked as "Sisters of the sacred well / That from beneath the seat of *Jove* doth spring"—a naming that includes the characteristic Miltonic account of origins. The next lines integrate the apotropaic movement into the invocation pattern:

Hence with denial vain, and coy excuse,
So may some gentle Muse
With lucky words favor my destin'd Urn,
And as he passes turn,
And bid fair peace be to my sable shrowd.

(18—22)

Here the metonymy of "Muse" for poet helps to prepare us for the later address to the "woful Shepherds" as Muse-figures. In addition, Milton sees the future poet "as he passes turn"—a phrase that portrays the future poet's movement through the transitory world ("as he passes") while it imagines his elegaic gesture of respect toward the earlier poet ("turn, / And bid fair peace be to my sable shrowd"). But, by now, we recognize the horizon of meanings surrounding this passing "turn." The word hints of the making of verse and the creation of harmony that Milton expects from his elegist; at the same time, on a deeper level, it seems to imagine and desire this future poet to make the same "turning" to which Milton's own elegy for King bears witness: the conversion of the poet to poetry. If for Milton "the act of creation is an act of choice, a turning, like a religious conversion, from the complexities of experience to the unity and direction of art,"[18] no other poem of his demands more of a renewal of the poet's faith. Milton rededicates himself to poetry even as he walks in the valley of the shadow of death, to mourn a fellow aspirant.

In "Lycidas" we have a text that "decides" a life. As at the end of the companion poems, the choice emerges in the realm of vocation, but where before he had only imagined potential identities and suspended the moment of decision, here he faces and survives the challenge, emerging with new faith: "To morrow to fresh Woods, and Pastures new." It is this process of constant renewal that great poetry demands, and it survives and triumphs over the greatest obstacles in the invocations of *Paradise Lost*, where the poet is still exploring "Pastures new":

Yet not the more
Cease I to wander where the Muses haunt
Clear Spring, or shadie Grove, or Sunnie Hill,
Smit with the love of sacred Song . . .

(III.26—29)

We are prepared for the great obstacles of "Lycidas" by the resistance implied in the very first words of the poem: "Yet once more . . ." The poem seems to begin as a response to a double threat: "Yet once more" reacts both to the thought "no more" and to the possibility "never again." In this sense, the poem's opening words contain an implied apotropaism, an overcoming of the double threat that *this* poem might not come into being and that this poem could be the last. The overcoming of the first threat is secured by the invocation to the Muses: "Hence with denial vain, and coy excuse." The triumph over the second threat (of "never again") is not at last achieved until the poem's final line, which almost seems a deliberate reply to this threat: "To morrow to fresh Woods, and Pastures new."

The second clear instance of invocation in "Lycidas" also adheres to the double pattern:

> O Fountain *Arethuse*, and thou honour'd floud,
> Smooth-sliding *Mincius*, crown'd with vocal reeds,
> That strain I heard was of a higher mood:
> But now my Oat proceeds . . .
>
>   (85 — 88)

The invocation here mediates another transition, the change in voice from Apollo's (heard in the immediately preceding passage, lines 76 — 84) to the poet's—thus confirming the general pattern of invocation as transition. The myth of Arethusa and Alpheus (earlier appearing in Milton's *Arcades*, lines 30 — 31) is essentially a Latin foundation myth for pastoral: the search for a new homeland for pastoral poetry. The invocation here of "*Arethuse*" and, later, of "*Alpheus*" (line 132) is appropriate to Milton's attempt, primarily through the strength of this very poem, to relocate the homeland of pastoral poetry in England. If Arethusa and Alpheus are the Muses of the poem's remaining two invocations, they are also Muses whose mythological associations exhibit clearly the mode and theme of the poem: transition and transfiguration (the two Miltonic versions of Ovidian metamorphosis). Each of them appears in the drama of the poem after an intervention by a higher voice: Arethusa, after the voice of Apollo; Alpheus, after the voice of St. Peter, "The Pilot of the Galilean lake" (line 109):

> But that two-handed engine at the door,
> Stands ready to smite once, and smite no more.
>   Return *Alpheus*, the dread voice is past
> That shrunk thy streams; Return *Sicilian* Muse,

And call the Vales, and bid them hither cast
Their Bells and Flourets of a thousand hues.

(130—35)

Invocation in "Lycidas" is rooted in the problem of transition from numinous voice to poetic voice. It is, in some measure, a response of the poet's human voice to the imagined presence of a divine voice, whether Apollo's or St. Peter's—corresponding to the encompassing divine voice of the Muse that inspires the entire poem. After this last invocation, the poet's voice quite naturally recedes into apostrophe —"Ye valleys low . . ."—thus confirming our sense that apostrophe and invocation exist along a common continuum. This final invocation of "Lycidas"—"Return *Alpheus*"—is, again, a doubled voice: ". . . Return *Sicilian* Muse." The name of Muse appearing in the second phrase serves to make explicit the identification of Alpheus and (retrospectively) Arethusa as true Muses, and this identification in turn only confirms that Milton himself conceived of these passages as invocations. The motif of the third invocation—"Return"—looks forward to similar themes in the third invocation of *Paradise Lost:* the return of the Muse ("Descend from Heav'n, *Urania,*" VII.1) and the relocation of the poet himself ("Return me to my Native Element," VII.16).

Early and late, Milton confronted the burden of the human mortality of the poet through the mediation of such figures as Lycidas and Orpheus. In elegy and epic, the third and final calling upon the Muse by name is dominated by imagery of voice. In "Lycidas" the poet asks, "Return *Alpheus*, the dread *voice* is past . . ." He bids the Muse to return and "*call* the Vales . . ." In short, the poet asks for the Muse's voice to substitute for the dread voice that has ended. In *Paradise Lost*, the poet follows the "Voice divine" (line 2) of Urania; he sings "with mortal voice" (line 24), surrounded by "evil tongues" (26), asking the Muse to expel "the barbarous dissonance" (32) of those whose "savage clamor" (36) drowned the "Harp and Voice" of Orpheus. Like its parallel in "Lycidas," the invocation is the response of "mortal voice" to "Voice divine." In each case, the summons of the poet to his Muse to return is in effect a final prayer for the completion of the poem.

In "Lycidas" the potential tragedy of voice is also mirrored in the myth of Orpheus:

What could the Muse her self that *Orpheus* bore,
The Muse her self for her inchanting son
Whom Universal nature did lament,
When by the rout that made the hideous roar,
His goary visage down the stream was sent,
Down the swift *Hebrus* to the *Lesbian* shore.[19]

(58—63)

If Orpheus is the Greek mythical figure who represents the poet as the human voice in its transcendent possibility, Apollo is the corresponding divine figure, representing the power and voice beyond the poet's reach. Thus, if Orpheus represents invocation, Apollo gives the image of vocation, the unexpected call:

But the fair Guerdon when we hope to find,
And think to burst out into sudden blaze,
Comes the blind *Fury* with th'abhorred shears,
And slits the thin-spun life. But not the praise,
Phoebus repli'd, and touch'd my trembling ears;
Fame is no plant that grows on mortal soil,
Nor in the glistering foil
Set off to th' world, nor in broad rumour lies,
But lives and spreds aloft by those pure eyes
And perfet witness of all-judging *Jove;*
As he pronounces lastly on each deed,
Of so much fame in Heav'n expect thy meed.

(73—84)

Here Milton consciously places himself in the pastoral mode of poetic ambition by deliberately echoing a passage in Vergil's "Sixth Eclogue," where Apollo reproves the young poet impatient to write an epic poem:

cum canerem reges et proelia, Cynthius aurem
vellit et admonuit: "pastorem, Tityre, pinguis
pascere oportet ovis, deductum dicere carmen."

(3—5)

When I was eager to sing of kings and battles
(i.e., to write an epic poem), Apollo plucked
my ear and warned: "A shepherd—Tityrus—
should feed sheep that are fat, but sing a
lay fine-spun."

(translation based on Loeb edition)

Milton's characteristic innovation is to expand the role of voice by dramatizing and revising the reply of Apollo, and his expanded version emphasizes the authority of the ultimate voice, that of Jove—"As he *pronounces* lastly on each deed." The allusion to Vergil only confirms the true consciousness of epic ambition in a poem where "the Muse her self" is Calliope, the Muse of epic poetry (lines 58−59).

The omnipresence of voice in "Lycidas" includes more than the various invocations, apostrophes, apotropaisms, and the dramatizations of voice—not only Apollo, but also Camus, St. Peter, and, finally, the "uncouth Swain" himself, whose voice is retrospectively seen to encompass almost the entire poem. It also includes the numerous examples of direct address: to the Nymphs, for example,

> Where were ye Nymphs when the remorseless deep
> Clos'd o're the head of your lov'd *Lycidas?*
>
> (50−51)

And to Lycidas himself:

> But O the heavy change, now thou art gon,
> Now thou art gon, and never must return!
> Thee Shepherd, thee the Woods, and desert Caves
> With wilde Thyme and the gadding Vine o'regrown,
> And all their echoes mourn.
>
> (37−41)

The "return" of Alpheus will, later in the poem, prepare the poet's true response to this earlier cry: "Now thou art gon, and never must return!" For the final movement of the poem is the true "return" of Lycidas, "sunk low, but mounted high" (line 172). And, as in the early cry of loss, the final triumph is expressed in a direct address to Lycidas:

> Now *Lycidas* the Shepherds weep no more;
> Henceforth thou art the Genius of the shore,
> In thy large recompense, and shalt be good
> To all that wander in that perilous flood.
>
> (182−85)

All of the patterns of voice in "Lycidas" combine to produce that particular effect of power, sustained through many changes, which readers of the poem have always felt and shared. Together, these patterns practically constitute the poem itself. The mystery of the Miltonic power of voice finds its most concentrated lyric example here, for in the poem Milton reveals voice in most of its various aspects: voice as invocation and as vocation, voice as the cry of loss and of redemption, and, in the future poem it contemplates ("So may some gentle Muse / With lucky words favour my destin'd Urn," lines 19—20), voice as influence. All these voices combine to effect a marvelous and lasting, mysterious catharsis for Milton and for the reader.

On the other side of this resonant elegy lay a profound silence. From "Lycidas" (1638) to *Paradise Lost* (1667) was a distance of almost thirty years during which no major poetic achievement appeared. Even the 1645 edition of the *Poems* becomes a retrospective testament to youthful promise.[20] The tomorrow promised by the elegy's final line was a far-off day, but the promise was continually renewed in the autobiographical passages of the prose works undertaken during this period. The silent poet interrupts "The Reason of Church Government" to assert: "Neither doe I think it a shame to covnant with any knowing reader, that for some few yeers yet I may go on trust with him toward the payment of what I am now indebted, as being a work not to be rays'd from the heat of youth."[21] Yet "the 'few years' for which Milton had covenanted with the knowing reader stretched to a quarter-century before that worthy's patience would be rewarded with *Paradise Lost*."[22] Milton's early complaint "But my late spring no bud or blossom shew'th" shadows the poet's entire career. In addition to vast labors undertaken, often apparently without effect, in defense of his moral and political ideals, Milton struggled endlessly with his choices for a proper epic subject and finally with the great epic labor itself: "long choosing, and beginning late" (IX.26). When *Paradise Lost* finally emerged, its invocations revealed a lyric intensity never before witnessed in the epic tradition—blossoming, as if in "late spring," from the long-buried seeds of Milton's lyrics—and a defense of inspiration in no way more impressively buttressed than by the poet's own seemingly miraculous creation of the first days of the world out of the dark abyss of his blind and aged solitude.

3 *Paradise Lost*

In Defense of Inspiration

The four invocations of *Paradise Lost*—at the beginning of Books I, III, VII, and IX—create and define an epic voice of extraordinary power. We, the readers, are lifted up into a great surge of narrative momentum by the first invocation, and each subsequent invocation recharges that energy in its own special way, while commenting on its own themes, recalling the themes of the epic or of past invocations, and building toward the future. These relationships form something like a substructure of epic forces, as they emanate from the story being told into the invocations and then back again to the themes and images of the epic. Perhaps in no other epic are the invocations so structurally significant, their language so resonant of the story's meaning.

Appreciation of the importance of Milton's epic invocations is the particular achievement of twentieth-century literary criticism. Before our century, their lyrical character was valued, but their structural importance was not understood. Except for the first invocation, Samuel Johnson considered them digressions, beautiful but irrelevant to the epic proper: "The short digressions at the beginning of the third, seventh, and ninth books, might doubtless be spared; but superfluities so beautiful, who would take away?"[1] The turning point in twentieth-century attitudes came with E. M. W. Tillyard's response to Johnson that the invocations "may be organic as well as beautiful in themselves. In point of fact they are a most valuable guide to the way the poem is constructed."[2] Structural and other aspects of these interior poems have since become the object of further studies, culminating in attempts to establish the invocations as a central focus of *Paradise Lost*.[3]

45

For the invocations not only mark important shifts in the epic; they define the epic voice that creates and maintains and interprets the narrative. The epic voice is an omniscient voice, one that claims to be inspired by a divine spirit. And the two epic claims of omniscience and divine inspiration are necessarily related, particularly in a book that imitates the Book of God. "The omniscient voice, after all, in order to be omniscient must either be divine, or inspired by divinity, or deluded into pretensions of divinity."[4] In this way the invocations present a crucial tension: Is divine inspiration a reality or a delusion? It is a tension again reflected in the story, as in the contrast between the truth of Michael's prophetic vision and the delusion of Eve's satanically inspired dream. Thus the invocations are searching meditations on the poetic power and on the powers of the divine spirit.

Milton's appeal to this spirit is, as we have seen, more than a conventional invoking of the Muse; nor is it merely an extension of his claim to be an omniscient narrator. It expresses, on its own terms, a theory of poetry that has grown out of his total poetic and religious experience from youth to manhood, but is here specifically applied to the great epic task before him. This is the last great defense of poetry in the Renaissance tradition, for all these prologues, taken together, constitute an eloquent defense of poetry as divine inspiration, a defense not of all poetry, but a defense of the kind of epic poetry Milton is now daring to write in *Paradise Lost*. To this extent, Milton's invocations express a notion of poetry that attempts to justify not only "God's ways to men," but also his own ways of writing about them. And this means not only a defense of poetry as divine inspiration, but also a defense of Christian epic as "not less but more heroic" than its predecessors.

The burden on Milton's shoulders was great: "From Petrarch's youth to Milton's age Europe awaited the poet and the poem which would demonstrate the equality of the modern age to antiquity. . . . . At issue . . . was the imaginative richness of the Christian religion."[5] Hence, if the invocations convey a sense of power, they also convey a peculiar anxiety because Milton has put himself totally on the line. Indeed, one factor in his choice of the epic mode over the purely dramatic presentation he earlier conceived may have been the need to emphasize the personal testamentary aspect of his poem: that it must be attested to by the responsible voice of one man who stands or falls by the truth of his utterance and his claim to be divinely inspired. This sense of the poem as testament implies a necessary limitation to the idea that the narrative voice is completely separable from Milton's own voice. Indeed the voice of the invocations is complex: intensely personal and yet ceremoniously impersonal at the same time. Its complexity is further revealed if we attempt to define its audience: Is the poet to justify God's ways to (all) men, as seems to be his resolve in the epic's opening? Or to the "fit audience" he hopes for at the center of his song? Or is—as one recent critic suggests—the "ultimate audience . . . God Himself"?[6] The poem's varying moods seem to allow us to say "yes" to all three questions, as indeed we would if they were asked of Eliot's *Four Quartets*, where, in language that is also both personal and ceremonial, the meditative poet, like the epic singer remembering Homer, recalls the image of the isolated Milton as he dwells on that fragmented time:

> If I think of a king at nightfall
> Of three men, and more, on the scaffold
> And a few who died forgotten
> In other places, here and abroad,
> And of one who died blind and quiet . . .
>
> ("Little Gidding")

But where we expect to find such meditations in a confessional poem such as the "Quartets," we do not expect them in an epic bard; and this odd combination of retrospective rumination and forward flight gives Milton's own interior passages one of their most memorable qualities.

Their bold style serves to create that special sense of awe appropriate to epic.[7] According to Tasso, indeed, epic's whole purpose is "moving the mind to wonder"[8] *(meraviglia)*, and if this is so, the boldness of Milton's first invocation may be seen as a conscious effort to create the epic mood in one stroke. Milton hardly can have been oblivious, too, of the long tradition that held that invocations themselves were "evidence of arrogance and presumption"[9]—a view held by Castelvetro, and criticized by Tasso. Tasso argues that the poet's trust in the divinity he invokes saves him from presumption, that there is a difference between pride and confidence, adding: "The ancient sophist Protagoras raised a similar objection against Homer, saying that his way of appealing to the Muse is peremptory, as if he meant to command her."[10]

Milton knows this peevish tradition of Castelvetro and flies in the face of it: "That with no middle flight intends to soar" *(Paradise Lost*

I. 14). He emphasizes his boldness and confidence, though he is also aware of the seductions of religious and poetic pride:

> Into the Heav'n of Heav'ns I have presum'd . . .
>
> (VII. 13)

Conscious of possible presumption, he finds reassurance in the fact that he is yet "Up led by thee," Urania (VII. 12). Soon, however, he reminds us of inherent dangers, and the mood changes from exaltation to fear:

> Least from this flying Steed unrein'd, (as once
> *Bellerophon*, though from a lower Clime)
> Dismounted, on th' *Aleian* Field I fall
> Erroneous there to wander and forlorne.
>
> (VII. 17−20)

Here "I fall" inevitably takes on a special meaning in keeping with the story—expressing fear that in this attempt to narrate the Fall of Man, Milton may reenact his own. The word appears again in the same invocation:

> . . . though fall'n on evil dayes,
> On evil dayes though fall'n, and evil tongues.
>
> (VII. 25−26)

Here again the poet seems to understand his own present situation in terms of a general condition: it is a contemporary and personal manifestation of the true story he is narrating. Milton and his contemporaries *are* fallen; and they perpetuate their fallen state by current strife.

The Fall provides an important context in which to examine Milton's attempt (and temptation) to write *Paradise Lost*, because he habitually placed man's effort to improve himself in that context. As he wrote in his "small tractate" "Of Education":

> The end then of learning is to repair
> the ruins of our first parents by regaining
> to know God aright . . .[11]

This statement may be extended to include his purpose in writing *Paradise Lost*. For its composition involved him in a process of self-education, just as today we, the readers, are educated by reading it.[12] The creation of *Paradise Lost*, as the invocation to Book III reminds

us, is a matter not only of discipline, but also of that divine illumination which, in the Augustinian tradition of Inner Light, is the guide
and tutor within us—what Augustine calls in the *De Trinitate* "the
indwelling Teacher."[13] To this teacher, the human, fallen creator of
Paradise Lost pays homage in the invocations, as he becomes educated
in his task of writing the poem, and it is to the instruction of this "holy
Light" (III.1) that he owes his own authority to instruct, even as the
heavenly Muse also inspired "That Shepherd, who first taught the
chosen Seed" (I.7−8).

ADVENTURES AND TEMPTATIONS

Milton's consciousness of his own fallen state and of the possibility of further temptation echoes throughout the poem. For instance,
the word *attempt* appears not only in the form of Milton's goal—
"Things unattempted yet in Prose or Rhime"; it also describes Satan's
project "to attempt the minde / of Man" (X.8−9). Both Satan and the
blind poet are about to *attempt* something in this epic, and Milton
experiences an undeniable *tempt*ation to achieve something of unprec-
edented grandeur.

Numerous other verbal reminiscences confirm the poet's interest
in key words of dual significance. In the first invocation, Milton
invokes the Muse's aid to his "adventrous Song." In its context the
word appropriately indicates both that his attempt is bold and that it is
an adventure, like the adventures of previous epics, though of a higher
kind—indicated just possibly by what may be a pun on the "advent" of
a new order or even on the Advent itself. But the word also appears
within the epic story. Adam tells Eve in Book IX, for instance, after he
has learned that she has eaten the fruit:

Bold deed thou hast presum'd, adventrous *Eve*.

(IX.921)

The Fall is thus, by implication, "adventrous," like Milton's epic
song. This implication is reinforced in "presum'd," which Milton, as
we have seen, uses to describe his epic attempt in the invocation to
Book VII.

The presumptuous potential of Milton's adventure is repeatedly
called to the reader's mind. The design of Sin and Death to build a road
from Hell to the New World is wittily called "Adventrous work" in

Book X (line 255). Later in the same book, Satan becomes a "great adventurer" (line 440) and describes his work in the New World as "my adventure" (468). Such parallels seem difficult to explain unless we suppose that Milton wishes us to grasp the whole truth of his situation, which includes the possibility that he may be reenacting his own fall in the attempt to write an epic about the Fall. His one hope lies in the reality of inspiration: "In creating his epic Milton, like Satan, is adventuring, questing over vast and illimitable spaces, but with this difference. Whereas Satan is always truly alone, defining all from within himself, the creative man looks outward spiritually and seeks divine light."[14] Both have "Escap't the *Stygian* Pool," but Milton recognizes the "sacred influence" (II.1,034) of light when it appears and, in trust, asks for its aid, whereas Satan makes what is by comparison an anti-invocation in Book IV:

> to thee I call,
> But with no friendly voice, and add thy name
> O Sun, to tell thee how I hate thy beams . . .
>
> (IV.35−37)

The distinguishing feature of Milton's boldness is thus its paradoxical humility. He "attempts" and "adventures" to stand or fall by a power that is not his own: "The essential message of Milton's epic invocations is . . . that everything, for the poet, depends upon his muse. The muse is both his support and justification. Such support, such justification is not commanded by the poet; rather it is sought by prayer, the efficacy of which must remain in doubt."[15]

One way of distinguishing among the four invocations is to measure the degree of confidence which Milton shows in relation to his dependence on the Muse. The first invocation is the most confident, almost as if it possessed certainty of the poem's completion.[16] Milton barely alludes to his blindness, except in the general metaphorical statement (which need not apply to blindness)

> What in me is dark
> Illumin . . .
>
> (I.22−23)

and in the allusion to "Siloa's Brook" (line 11).[17] And this latter allusion only underscores the triumphant mood by referring to the divine curing of a blind man in John:

And as Jesus passed by, he saw a man which was blind from
his birth. And his disciples asked him, saying, Master, who
did sin, this man, or his parents, that he was born blind?
Jesus answered, Neither hath this man sinned, nor his
parents: but that the works of God should be made manifest
in him . . . he anointed the eyes of the blind man with the
clay, and said unto him, Go, wash in the pool of
Siloam . . . He went his way, therefore, and washed, and
came seeing.

$$(9:1-7)$$

The allusion is richly suggestive both of the divine efficacy in bringing
Milton true vision and of his ultimate innocence. The story of John
continues by showing the harassment the cured man received from the
Pharisees. Perhaps this also was present in Milton's mind, but if so he
waits until the prologue of Book VII to depict it. In any event, this first
invocation summons all the energies, divine and human, that Milton
will need in the telling of *Paradise Lost.*

Imagery is also introduced that will be developed and refined
through the other invocations. The poet's song, for example, is like a
bird—like an eagle, perhaps, when it looks directly into the source of
light—"That with no middle flight intends to soar." In the invocation
to Book III, this image returns:

Thee I re-visit now with bolder wing

$$(III.13)$$

And the poet seems now to remember another bird, the lyrical nightingale:

as the wakeful Bird
Sings darkling, and in shadiest Covert hid
Tunes her nocturnal Note.

$$(III.38-40)$$

In the last passage bird and blind singer seem to fuse, the "blind singer"
being the other significant image of the invocation to Book III,[18]
whose main subject is the paradox of vision granted to a blind man "that
the works of God should be made manifest in him" (John 9:3). If the
bird images Milton's aspiration, the blind bard perhaps images the
inspiration that makes his aspiration possible. The mood of the Book

III invocation is a complex intertwining of varying moments: rever-
ent, searching, suppliant, lamenting, troubled but resolved, deter-
mined and humble. There is a great compression of nuance and
allusion in its fifty-five lines. The interior sense of time seems
extended, because so much is suggested, revolved, considered, medi-
tated.

Again there are verbal and thematic reminiscences of the Fall, of
satanic overreaching. In Book IX, when Satan is tempting Eve, he
experiences an inspiration that is almost a parody of the invocation to
Book III:

> Hope elevates, and joy
> Bright'ns his Crest, as when a wandring Fire . . .
> Hovering and blazing with delusive Light,
> Misleads th' amaz'd Night-wanderer from his way
> To Boggs and Mires, and oft through Pond or Poole,
> There swallow'd up and lost, from succour farr.
> (IX.633−34; 639−42)

The passage is a striking reminder of Milton's imagery in presenting
his own situation. The misled, lost Night-*wanderer* following a
wandering fire seems to be the satanic shadow cast by Milton's own
heroic dedication to the Muse: "Yet not the more / Cease I to *wander*
. . ." (III.26−27). Here the verb *wander* is used to suggest the
freedom and fulfillment experienced in poetic dedication. Its meaning
is further enriched by its use in describing Eden:

> That Earth now
> Seemed like to Heav'n, a seat where Gods might dwell,
> Or wander with delight, and love to haunt
> Her sacred shades . . .
> (VII.328−31)

Again the verbal similarities are so close that each passage might be
adduced to gloss the other. We are left with the impression that
Milton's poetic dedication endows him with an almost divine freedom
and delight and grants to his blind eyes a vision of paradise restored. At
the same time, however, like *attempt*, and *adventrous*, *wander* has its
demonic connotation in "Night-wanderer" and its connotations of the
Fall, as when Adam blames the Fall on Eve's "pride / And wandring
vanitie" (X.874−75), or when Eve laments her banishment from
Paradise,

> from thee
> How shall I part, and whither wander down
> Into a lower World . . . ?
>
> (XI.281−83)

The risks and dangers of creative aspiration that are suggested by these reminiscences form the major theme of the invocation to Book VII, where Milton has ventured half way toward his goal. He now implores a christened Urania not only for continued inspiration, but also for safety in his astronomical adventure:

> Up led by thee
> Into the Heav'n of Heav'ns I have presum'd
> An Earthlie Guest, and drawn Empyreal Aire,
> Thy tempring; with like saftie guided down
> Return me to my Native Element:
> Least from this flying Steed unrein'd, (as once
> *Bellerophon,* though from a lower Clime)
> Dismounted, on th' *Aleian* Field I fall
> Erroneous there to wander and forlorne.
>
> (VII.12−20)

While "Half yet remaines unsung," Milton experiences a fear of abandonment and disaster, expressed in the fallen prototype of Bellerophon, whose forlorn wandering in the Aleian Field may be contrasted to the poet's delightful and protected wandering among the Muses' haunts described in the previous invocation (III.27). Bellerophon's attempt to explore the heavens on Pegasus provides a mythical identification for Milton in this invocation, like the bird and blind singer in the previous one. Milton is already abandoned on earth

> In darkness, and with dangers compast round,
> And solitude.
>
> (VII.27−28)

His most fervent hope can now be expressed only in the negative terms that the Muse must *not fail* him:

> So fail not thou, who thee implores.
>
> (VII.38)

A second myth—that of Orpheus—also recalls the tragic and horrid effects of abandonment; the "*Thracian* Bard," violently dismembered, and his harmony drowned, excites the singer's worst fear: "nor could the Muse defend / Her Son" (VII.37—38). The invocation vividly shows the poet in a state of alienation, feeling threatened both in his earthly environment and within himself, imploring his Muse, but remembering keenly a Muse that proved of no avail.

In the invocation to Book IX, Milton seems to take for granted all that he has established in the previous invocations. He even begins without a formal address.[19] His mood seems almost impatient now, certainly more austere, as he snaps

> No more of talk where God or Angel Guest
> With Man, as with his Friend, familiar us'd
> To sit indulgent . . .
>
> (IX.1—3)

In a similar mood he tosses aside the "less heroic" stories of his classical predecessors:

> Of stern *Achilles* on his Foe pursu'd
> Thrice Fugitive about *Troy* Wall; or rage
> Of *Turnus* for *Lavinia* disespous'd,
> Or *Neptun's* ire or *Juno's*, that so long
> Perplex'd the *Greek* and *Cytherea's* Son.
>
> (IX.15—19)

When he sums up the achievement of previous heroic poetry, now including medieval and Renaissance story as well, he finds that its chief mastery was

>   to dissect
> With long and tedious havoc fabl'd Knights
> In Battels feign'd . . .
>
> (IX.29—31)

He interjects, in what might seem to be an advertisement for *Samson Agonistes,*

>   the better fortitude
> Of Patience and Heroic Martyrdom
> Unsung . . .
>
> (IX.31—33)

His remark even recalls to us the language of that drama:

> Extolling Patience as the truest fortitude . . .

> But Patience is more oft the exercise
> Of Saints, the trial of thir fortitude . . .

> Whom Patience finally must crown.
>   *(Samson Agonistes,* 654; 1,287−88; 1,296)

The story of Samson is of course a biblical story, like that of *Paradise Lost;* in both works the poet chooses to imitate the Book of God. When Milton claims superiority to "fabl'd Knights / In Battels feign'd," the words *fabled* and *feigned* give us the clue to his principal claim to superiority. Milton claims to imitate the divine truth, beside which all other stories are suspect. And this claim seems to support the prologue's bold examination of the nature of true heroism:

> that which justly gives Heroic name
> To Person or to Poem.
>
>   (IX.40−41)

Although false conceptions of heroism have been ruthlessly exposed in the preceding lines (15−19, 33−39), Milton does not elaborate on this final utterance. The clear implication is that the answer is writ large in the poem he is now composing: in the Son's offer of himself as Example; in Satan's adventure as counterexample;[20] or in Abdiel's defiance, or Adam and Eve's rededication to mankind, or even in Milton's own heroism as a poet, vividly portrayed in the invocations themselves.

Discussions of who is the true hero of the epic usually tend to be quite partisan, possibly missing the richness of what seems Milton's open-ended implication here that the entire poem in various ways contributes to a deeper understanding of heroism.

Whereas the previous invocations prayerfully implored the Muse, in this last invocation she is unimplored. For she now visits him without his asking:

> my Celestial Patroness, who deignes
> Her nightly visitation unimplor'd.
>
>   (IX.21−22)

This is a marked contrast to his previous situation:

> So fail not thou, who thee implores.
>
> (VII.38)

Now the Muse

> dictates to me slumbring, or inspires
> Easie my unpremeditated Verse.
>
> (IX.23−24)

Yet even this invocation does not show the balanced and sustained assurance of the first one. It ends poignantly, with a resurgence of fears that are calmed in the end only by the thought that the source of his inspiration will continue. His trust is now with the divine power and the inherent strength of the true heroic subject that he has defended in this invocation:

> higher Argument
> Remaines, sufficient of it self to raise
> That name, unless an age too late, or cold
> Climat, or Years damp my intended wing
> Deprest, and much they may, if all be mine,
> Not Hers who brings it nightly to my Ear.
>
> (IX.42−7)

INTENDED WINGS

The placement of the invocations appears to be related to the epic story's structure, compared by one of the best of the poem's critics to an inverted V: "We begin at the lowest point, we end at a point not quite so low, but far below the heights to which we have soared in the middle. Within this basic structure are a number of smaller patterns where lesser ascents and descents are followed. The whole is a great vision of rising and falling action." This structure is reinforced by verbal texture: "A diagram of the skeleton of *Paradise Lost* can give no idea of the extent to which we are made conscious, in the poem's verbal texture, of the structure's basic dimensions of depth and height, and the corresponding movements downward or upward. *Rise* and *raise, fall, high* and *height, low, deep* and *depth*, variations like *aspire* and *descend*, and the adverbs of direction, are repeated literally hundreds of times."[21]

Now if we divide the epic into two halves, we see that the invocations appear to be symmetrically arranged, such that the pattern of placement of the first half is exactly followed in the second half. This can be simply illustrated:

I Invocation	......	VII Invocation
II		VIII
III Invocation	......	IX Invocation
IV		X
V		XI
VI		XII

If we focus specifically on certain thematic and imagistic relationships in the invocations and keep in mind the idea of rising and falling action, this structure assumes even greater significance:

I INVOCATION

a. Announces the
   "poetic" ascent:
   "That with no middle
   flight intends
   to soar"

b. Prays for "aid" in
   the poetic ascent

c. The inspired ascent
   of Moses (to Mount Sinai)

VII INVOCATION

a. Announces the
   "poetic" descent:
   "Descend from
   Heav'n, *Urania*"
   "Return me . . ."

b. Prays for "saftie" in
   the poetic descent

c. The threatening descent
   of Bellerophon (to
   the Aleian Field)

III INVOCATION

a. Announces the
   poet's own reascent:
   "and up to reascend,
   Though hard
   and rare"

b. Prologue to Satan's
   ascent (to Mount Niphates)

c. Prologue to God's
   defense of Man's
   freedom (potential)
   to fall

IX INVOCATION

a. Announces Man's descent
   (Fall): "I now must
   change / Those Notes
   to Tragic"

b. Prologue to Man's descent
   ("to the subjected
   Plaine")

c. Prologue to Man's
   (actual) Fall and
   doubts of God's
   wisdom

In addition to these correspondences, we have seen the importance of Book IX as a whole in informing the verbal texture of the invocation to Book III, as for example the "delusive Light" of Satan's inspiration (IX.639) in relation to the poet's "holy Light" (III.1).

The structural relationship of the four invocations is thus a doubled progression in which both sides mirror one another, but move in opposing directions. But this view presents only one of the perspectives. For there is a sense in which the progression toward more secure inspiration from the invocation in Book III to the one in Book IX circles back to the invocation in Book I, the most confident of the four.[22] The first invocation assumes a completed poem, an answered prayer. Both progressive and circular patterns seem to exist together, but both are necessarily partial visions of the ultimate structure of the poem's invocations.

THE PASTORAL VISION

We must not forget—whatever our geometrical metaphor for their structure—that the invocations are "carefully spaced so that we never lose sight of this human composer," who brings all together before our eyes. For a major function of the invocations, it has been emphasized, is "to remind us, ultimately, that this poem is an action of thoughts within a central controlling intelligence that moves with inward eyes toward a recovery of Paradise."[23] If Milton *dares* like Satan, he also *names* and *sings* like unfallen Adam; always he is a poet whose inner light illuminates a pastoral landscape of Eden-like freedom:

> where the Muses haunt
> Cleer Spring, or shadie Grove, or Sunnie Hill . . .
> (III.27−28)

When the blind poet thinks of light, he thinks of those precious things that light illuminates—

> the sweet approach of Ev'n or Morn
> Or sight of vernal bloom, or Summers Rose,
> Or flocks, or heards, or human face divine . . .
> (III.42−44)

—residuals of an unfallen world that, though it no longer exists, he can image in the light of his verse. The pastoral evocation of "flocks,"

"heards," even "human face divine" and of "Cleer Spring, or shadie
Grove, or Sunnie Hill" has a particular force in a poem whose center is
the Ur-pastoral vision: the vision of Eden.[24] Natural light evokes the
pastoral landscape, and the divine light of inspiration enables the fallen
poet to create, in images of pastoral poetry, the Eden that man has lost:

> Thus was this place,
> A happy rural seat of various view;
> Groves whose rich Trees wept odorous Gumms and
> Balme,
> Others whose fruit burnisht with Golden Rinde
> Hung amiable, *Hesperian* Fables true,
> If true, here only, and of delicious taste:
> Betwixt them Lawns, or level Downs, and Flocks
> Grasing the tender herb, were interpos'd,
> Or palmie hilloc, or the flourie lap
> Of som irriguous Valley spred her store,
> Flours of all hue, and without Thorn the Rose:
> Another side, umbrageous Grots and Caves
> Of coole recess, o're which the mantling vine
> Layes forth her purple Grape, and gently creeps
> Luxuriant; mean while murmuring waters fall
> Down the slope hills, disperst, or in a Lake,
> That to the fringed Bank with Myrtle crownd,
> Her chyrstal mirror holds, unite thir streams.
> The Birds thir quire apply; aires, vernal aires,
> Breathing the smell of field and grove, attune
> The trembling leaves, while Universal *Pan*
> Knit with the *Graces* and the *Hours* in dance
> Led on th' Eternal Spring.

> (IV.246−68)

In Eden, as in the invocation to Book III, light is the nourishing
source that makes possible the pastoral landscape, where Milton implicitly identifies himself with Adam. We can see the importance of
light and its relation to the pastoral world as Adam describes his birth
and awakening to Raphael:

> As new wak't from soundest sleep
> Soft on the flourie herb I found me laid
> In Balmie Sweat, which with his Beames the Sun

Soon dri'd, and on the reaking moisture fed.
Strait toward Heav'n my wondring Eyes I turnd,
And gaz'd a while the ample Skie, till rais'd
By quick instinctive motion up I sprung,
As thitherward endevoring, and upright
Stood on my feet; about me round I saw
Hill, Dale, and shadie Woods, and sunnie Plaines,
And liquid Lapse of murmuring Streams; by these,
Creatures that liv'd, and mov'd, and walk'd, or flew,
Birds on the branches warbling; all things smil'd . . .
                                        (VIII.253−65)

He intuits immediately the central importance of the sun, as his first
words show; they in fact constitute a "poetic invocation" recalling the
invocation to Book III with its images of the sun lighting up the
pastoral world:

Thou Sun, said I, faire Light,
And thou enlight'nd Earth, so fresh and gay,
Ye Hills and Dales, ye Rivers, Woods, and Plaines,
And ye that live and move, fair Creatures, tell . . .
                                        (VIII.273−76)

Just as the sun enlightens earth, so Milton's divine source of light,
"holy Light," allows him a restoring vision of a world unfallen as he
"moves with inward eyes toward a recovery of Paradise." The pastoral
vision is a source of renewal that, like Siloa's Brook, makes the blind
man see.

In Eden, Adam and Eve offer every morning their hymn of
adoration and praise to their Maker:

. . . in fit strains pronounc't or sung
Unmeditated, such prompt eloquence
Flowd from their lips, in Prose or numerous Verse,
More tuneable then needed Lute or Harp
To add more sweetness, and they thus began.
These are thy glorious works . . .
                                        (V.148−53)

"Unmeditated" like Milton's song, the hymn they sing, as has often
been noted, contains numerous reminiscences of the Psalms: "Adam,
in his garden paradise, stands at the beginning as the forerunner of

David, the hebraic pastoral singer."[25] Similarly, in his harmonizing control of nature, Adam is possibly to be taken as forerunner of Orpheus and of pagan poetry:

> As thus he spake, each Bird and Beast behold
> Approaching two and two, These cowring low
> With blandishment, each Bird stoop'd on his wing.
> I nam'd them, as they pass'd, and understood
> Thir Nature . . .
>
> (VIII.349–53)

Perhaps he is even the prototype of Solomon, the love poet, who whispers to Eve

> Awake
> My fairest, my espous'd, my latest found,
> Heav'ns last best gift, my ever new delight,
> Awake, the morning shines, and the fresh field
> Calls us . . .
>
> (V.17–21)

an invitation echoing the Song of Solomon:

> My beloved spake, and said unto me,
> Rise up, my love, my fair one, and come away . . .
>
> (2:10)

Adam is not only the first man; he is the first singer. He makes, as we have seen, the first poetic invocation:

> Thou Sun, said I, faire Light . . .
>
> (VIII.273)

For Milton, this light is both a reminder of the lost Eden and a promise of the paradise within. Thus the invocation to Book III resonates not only with satanic echoes of Milton's daring attempt, but also with echoes of paradise and the promise of restoration.

Though in the Fall the original innocence of Adam's songs is lost, their image is recreated in the heroic effort of Milton's verse, straining interior vision toward the recovery of Eden. At the end of the invocation to "holy Light," Milton implores

> So much the rather thou Celestial light
> Shine inward, and the mind through all her powers

> Irradiate, there plant eyes, all mist from thence
> Purge and disperse, that I may see and tell
> Of things invisible to mortal sight.

(III.51 — 55)

In asking the Light to "plant eyes," the poet fuses images of both light and Eden in a single hope: that his vision may become the seed from which the restored garden springs.

4 Voice and Crisis

MILTON AND THE PSALMS

I in the day of my distress
Will call on thee for aid.
Ps. 86:7
As translated by Milton

Adam and Eve's "Unmeditated" song of praise and adoration in the garden is, in a sense, the ideal invocation of *Paradise Lost*. It is the unfallen model of Milton's own "unpremeditated Verse." The voice of our first parents rises out of the morning landscape, as the sun itself rises over the earth:

Discovering in wide Lantskip all the east
Of Paradise and *Edens* happie Plains,
Lowly they bow'd adoring, and began
Thir Orisons, each Morning duly paid
In various style, for neither various style
Nor holy rapture wanted they to praise
Thir Maker, in fit strains pronounc't or sung
Unmeditated, such prompt eloquence
Flowd from thir lips, in Prose or numerous Verse,
More tuneable then needed Lute or Harp
To add more sweetness, and they thus began.
    These are thy glorious works, Parent of good,
Almightie, thine this universal Frame,
Thus wondrous fair; thy self how wondrous then!
Unspeakable, who sitst above these Heavens

63

To us invisible or dimly seen
In these thy lowest works, yet these declare
Thy goodness beyond thought, and Power Divine.
                                        (V. 142−59)

As many have recognized, the beginning of their hymn is an intricate
variation on the Psalms, upon one in particular:

The heavens declare the glory of God;
and the firmament sheweth his handywork.
Day unto day uttereth speech,
and night unto night sheweth knowledge.
There is no speech nor language,
where their voice is not heard.
                                        (Ps. 19:1−3)

A close comparison of the two passages will show the difficulty—and
the triumph—of Milton's art, aspiring to recreate the sublime character even of Scripture's most celebrated passages. Milton's reworking of
the psalm through the dramatic voice of Adam and Eve comes to us as
his own meditative reinterpretation and also as original event, returning in spirit to the source of divine inspiration that moved the original
singer. The hymn continues:

Speak yee who best can tell, ye Sons of light,
Angels, for yee behond him, and with songs
And choral symphonies, Day without Night,
Circle his Throne rejoycing, yee in Heav'n,
On Earth joyn all ye Creatures to extoll
Him first, him last, him midst, and without end.
                                        (V. 160−65)

Our parents' psalm, searching through the whole creation to celebrate
the morning star (lines 166−70), the sun (171−74), moon (175−
76), planets (177−79), air (line 180), the elements (180−84), the
"Mists" and "showers" (185−91), the winds and trees (192−96), and
finally "all ye living Souls," the animals of all kinds (lines 197−204),
extends the biblical base of Adam and Eve's invocation, for its design is
an elaborate variation on Psalm 148:

Praise ye him, all his angels:
praise ye him, all his hosts

Praise ye him, sun and moon:
praise him, all ye stars of light . . .
   Fire, and hail; snow, and vapours;
stormy wind fulfilling his word:
   Mountain, and all hills;
fruitful trees, and all cedars:
   Beasts, and all cattle;
creeping things, and flying fowl:

                              (2−3, 8−10)

Adam and Eve then proceed to a psalm-like declaration of loyalty in a
spirit that some have felt is Milton's own, "Witness if I be silent" (line
202)[1] and conclude with the request that "if the night / Have gather'd
ought of evil or conceal'd, / Disperse it, as now light dispels the dark"
(lines 206−8). These last lines seem striking as an echo of Milton's
own words at the end of the invocation to light:

            . . . all mist from thence
   Purge and disperse. . . .
                              (III.53−54)

Yet they too are based on the psalmist's familiar cry to "purge" (Ps.
51:7, 65:3, 79:9) and disperse "all mine enemies" (Ps. 3:7 and 6:10,
for example), enemies that may be either inside or outside the soul.
The theme, however, is uncharacteristic of the psalms of praise; it
reflects the psalms of distress, and reminds us of the threat to happiness
revealed in Eve's "troublesome dream" of the night just passed.[2]
   Though it was Milton's conviction in the composition of
Paradise Lost that the Bible provides forms of expression at least as
powerful as those inherited from the classics,[3] the possibility of a
psalmist context for the invocations in that poem has not been as deeply
explored as we might expect in view of the poet's own lifelong interest
in the Psalms and the general seventeenth-century preoccupation with
translating them and setting them to music.[4] Milton's father, for
example, had supplied tunes for five psalms in Ravenscroft's 1621
psalter.[5] Sidney, less than a generation before Milton's birth, had
begun a project of translating the entire canon[6]—an effort in which
dozens of writers would eventually play a part, from genuine poets such
as Wither, Sandys, Carew, Crashaw, and Vaughan, to the rhyming
teams Steinhold and Hopkins, Tate and Brady. By the time of Milton's
invocations, the Psalms had become part of an English literary tradi-

tion as well as of the European tradition of religious meditation. In a strain, in fact, similar to Sidney's in the *Apology*, Milton had praised the Psalms along with other poetry of the Old Testament as history's highest lyrical achievement; in *The Reason of Church Government*, at the end of his famous review of possible models for his own ambitious plans, "though of highest hope, and hardest attempting," he examines "those magnifick Odes and Hymns wherein *Pindarus* and *Callimachus* are in most things worthy" and then concludes: "But those frequent songs throughout the law and prophets beyond all these, not in their divine argument alone, but in the very critical art of composition, may be easily made appear over all the kinds of Lyrick poesy, to be incomparable."[7]

THE VERY CRITICAL ART OF COMPOSITION

The earliest known poetic exercise by Milton is a paraphrase of Psalm 114. His formal education from grammar school through university was involved with the Psalms as basic texts for memorization; and in the Hebrew studies pursued at St. Paul's and Cambridge, there is every reason to believe he would have become acquainted even with Hebrew versification.[8] It seems probable, in fact, that the "critical art" he claims for the Psalms includes not only the familiar parallelism-within-variation, which in *Paradise Lost* he makes so prominent a feature of his own style, but certain configurations of structure as well. The so-called "Lament Psalms," for instance, have been shown by recent scholarship to contain always four elements: "(a) a brief invocation of God, often no more than the divine name; (b) a cry for hearing and help; (c) a statement of the nature and causes of the misfortune; and (d) a prayer for deliverance."[9] Adam and Eve's appeal for deliverance from potential evil in their morning hymn of course is based on this last motif, and Milton makes it stand out further, for his narrative purposes, by devoting the entire hymn up to that point to uninterrupted praise.

In ancient Israel, Lament Psalms "were sung both by individuals during personal crises and by the community in times of national disaster."[10] In a general sense, Milton's invocations are similar documents, showing traces of both personal and national suffering, having been composed during what Milton could only regard as a prolonged "national disaster." Furthermore, if Milton's middle years seem generally a period of delay in his epic mission, the years 1641 − 50 show an almost total poetic eclipse with one exception—and the exception is instructive:

> In the spring of 1648 he translated nine psalms. He had paraphrased or translated two psalms when he was fifteen, and had done one into Greek in 1637; otherwise he had shown no interest in such work. Now he translates nine psalms, and in 1653 eight more. Why would he have taken up this work at this juncture? Is it not because, after the long intermission, the long silences, he was trying to renew his dedication as God's poet, trying to rekindle his sense of inspiration?[11]

The translations of 1653 are Milton's last known translations of the Psalms. On seven successive days (Aug. 8 − 14), he translated Psalms 2 to 8 (Psalm 1 is *"Done into Verse,* 1653," with the exact date unspecified). Most of these (five of the eight) are Lament Psalms, and the translations show him groping already in the stylistic direction of *Paradise Lost* and its epic invocations, where the themes of the Lament Psalms will be interwoven with the other psalmist themes of praise, thanks, confidence, and long-suffering. By comparing his translations to those of the King James Version (which served as his family Bible), we can glimpse something of their expression of a pattern of thought and feeling that will recur in the invocations. The most interesting passage for this purpose is the poet's elaboration of Ps. 6:7. Here the King James Version has

> Mine eye is consumed because of grief;
> it waxeth old because of all mine enemies.

Milton expands and revises the thought:

> . . . mine Eie
> Through grief consumes, is waxen old and dark
> Ith' mid'st of all mine enemies that mark.
> (Milton's translation, 13 − 15)

Capitalizing "Eie," the newly blind Milton speaks from an experience of the "dark" that is to be transformed but not relieved when it surfaces again in the invocation to light. His eye, moreover grows "old and

dark" not, as in the King James Version "*because* of all mine enemies,"
but "*Ith' midst* of all mine enemies *that mark*." The location is
interesting because, in a way altogether characteristic of a blind man, it
assumes the stance of the embattled singer in the invocation to Book
VII. Already his enemies surround him, eye him, take aim at him.

Similarly premonitory is Milton's version of Psalm 3:

> How many those
> That in arms against me rise;
> Many are they
> That of my life distrustfully thus say,
> No help for him in God there lies.
>
> . . .
>
> of many millions
> The populous rout
> I fear not though incamping round about
> They pitch against me their Pavillions.
>   (Milton's translation, 2−6, 15−18)

In a few years, Milton will urge the Muse in *Paradise Lost* to expel
"that wilde Rout that tore the *Thracian* Bard," bringing together
(perhaps) in a single image the situations of the mythic poet of
antiquity and the historical poet of the psalter. The King James
Version merely says, "I will not be afraid of ten thousands of people,
that have set themselves against me round about" (Ps. 3:6). From the
lonely position of the beleaguered blind man, the "thousands" multiply
fast. The metaphor of threatened dismemberment in the Orpheus
passage is itself a frequent psalmist convention. In his translation of the
seventh psalm, Milton interprets the psalmist's fear of his enemy in a
way wholly characteristic both of him and his original:

> Least as a Lion (and no wonder)
> He hast to tear my Soul asunder
> Tearing and no rescue nigh.
>   (Milton's translation, 4−6)

The experience of helplessness here, ending with "and no rescue
nigh," seems already to be reaching for the cadence of his commentary
on the Orpheus story: "nor could the Muse defend / Her Son."[12] Fear
of dismemberment, moreover, is only one aspect of the psalmist's
imagery of lament. Variously he externalizes his situation by picturing

himself "in the grip of death, drowning in the sea, slipping into the underworld, entangled in the hunter's net, mired in a bog, or torn to pieces by savage beasts,"[13] and some of these same images appear, though perhaps only coincidentally and certainly with coloring from other traditions, in *Paradise Lost's* invocations: "the *Stygian* Pool" (III.13) from which the poet escapes, his "dark descent" (III.20) into the underworld, the imagined drowning of "Harp and Voice" (VII.37), and the self-portrait of entanglement in the disasters of the times: "fall'n on evil dayes . . . and evil tongues . . . In darkness, and with dangers compast round" (VII.25−27). One does not need the Psalms to account for any of these, yet it would not surprise us to discover, with reference to any or all of them, that classical and biblical archetypes are here again, as so often in Milton's imagination, submerged and merged.

Milton's deep experience of the Psalms seems to be implicit not only in some aspects of the poetic texture of the invocations but also in the structure. Let us, for example, reexamine systematically the four parts of the Lament Psalm with respect to Milton's texts:

(1) *"a brief invocation of God, often no more than the divine name"*:

Sing Heav'nly Muse . . . (I.6)

And chiefly Thou O Spirit . . . (I.17)

Hail holy Light . . . (III.1)

thou Celestial light . . . (III.51)

Descend from Heav'n *Urania* . . . (VII.1)

still govern thou my Song, / *Urania* . . . (VII.30−31)

(2) *"a cry for hearing and help"*:

      I thence
Invoke thy aid to my adventrous Song (I.12−13)

Instruct me, for Thou know'st . . . (I.19)

      What in me is dark
Illumin, what is low raise and support . . . (I.22−23)

May I express thee unblam'd? (III.3)

> . . . thou Celestial light
Shine inward . . . (III.51—52)

Return me to my Native Element . . . (VII.16)

> still govern thou my Song,
Urania, and fit audience find, though few. (VII.30—31)

But drive farr off the barbarous dissonance . . . (VII.32)

So fail not thou, who thee implores . . . (VII.38)

(3) *"a statement of the nature and causes of the misfortune"* (There are at least two "misfortunes" in this context: the generic one of the Fall, the subject of the epic, which includes the poet's own fallenness, and the individual one of Milton's blindness, isolation, and personal danger after the Stuart Restoration):

> Of Man's First Disobedience, and the Fruit
Of that Forbidden Tree, whose mortal tast
Brought Death into the World, and all our woe,
With loss of *Eden* . . . (I.1—4)

> . . . but thou
Revisit'st not these eyes, that rowle in vain
To find thy piercing ray, and find no dawn;
So thick a drop serene hath quencht thir Orbs,
Or dim suffusion veild. (III.22—26)

> Thus with the Year
Seasons return, but not to me returns
Day, or the sweet approach of Ev'n or Morn,
Or sight of vernal bloom, or Summers Rose,
Or flocks, or heards, or human face divine;
But cloud in stead, and ever-during dark
Surrounds me, from the chearful wayes of men
Cut off, and for the Book of knowledge fair
Presented with a Universal blanc
Of Natures works to mee expung'd and ras'd,
And wisdome at one entrance quite shut out. (III.40—50)

> . . . fall'n on evil dayes,
On evil dayes though fall'n, and evil tongues;
In darkness, and with dangers compast round,

And solitude . . . (VII.25—28)

(4) *"a prayer for deliverance":*

Restore us . . . (I.5)

So much the rather thou Celestial light
Shine inward, and the mind through all her powers
Irradiate, there plant eyes, all mist from thence
Purge and disperse, that I may see and tell
Of things invisible to mortal sight. (III.51—55)

      . . . with like saftie guided down
Return me to my Native Element:
Least from this flying Steed unrein'd, (as once
Bellerophon, though from a lower Clime)
Dismounted, on th' *Aleian* Field I fall
Erroneous there to wander and forlorne. (VII.15—20)

But drive farr off the barbarous dissonance
Of *Bacchus* and his revellers, the Race
Of that wilde Rout that tore the *Thracian* Bard
In *Rhodope,* where Woods and Rocks had Eares
To rapture, till the savage clamor dround
Both Harp and Voice . . . (VII.32—37)

Milton's powerfully compressive and allusive imagination has unmistakably fused the predominant motif of the final passage—Orpheus's dismemberment—with the psalmist context, for "Harp and Voice" (VII.37) are primary attributes of both:

    Sing unto the Lord with the harp; with
the harp, and the voice of a psalm.
                        (Ps. 98:5)

    The above scenario seems to indicate the presence of all essential aspects of the Lament Psalm in the invocations of *Paradise Lost.* Beyond that, however, the characteristic psalm dwells on the idea of invocation and opens with one:

    Hear me when I call, O God of my righteousness . . .
                        (Ps. 4:1)

    Give ear to my words, O Lord,

Consider my meditation.
Hearken unto the voice of my cry, my King, and my God:
My voice shalt thou hear in the morning, O Lord;
In the morning will I direct my prayer unto thee . . .
(Ps. 5:1−3)

I will praise thee, O Lord, with my whole heart . . .
(Ps. 9:1)

Lord, I cry unto thee: make haste unto me;
Give ear unto my voice, when I cry unto thee.
(Ps. 141:1)

What these quotations and dozens more that might be chosen show us is that the intent of invocation in the Psalms is to announce the singer's presence to the power he invokes, and his awareness of the shadow of absence out of which he speaks. Throughout the Psalms, in fact, imageries of voice create the drama of man's speech (and ways) grappling with God's:

The heavens declare the glory of God;
and the firmament sheweth his handywork.
Day unto day uttereth speech,
and night unto night sheweth knowledge.
There is no speech nor language,
where their voice is not heard.
(Ps. 19:1−3)

The voice of the Lord is upon the waters:
The God of glory thundereth: . . .
The voice of the Lord is powerful;
The voice of the Lord is full of majesty;
The voice of the Lord divideth the flames of fire.
The voice of the Lord shaketh the wilderness.
(Ps. 29:3−4, 7−8)

Man's supplicating voice seeks to convert absence into presence:

Let my prayer come before thee . . .
(Ps. 88:2)

and ultimate alienation expresses itself in the imagery of the voice that is not heard:

My God, my God, why hast thou forsaken me?
Why art thou so far from helping me, and from the
    words of my roaring?
O my God, I cry in the daytime, but thou hearest not.

(Ps. 22:1—2)

These manifestations of voice in the Psalms are significant for any attempt to discover the fullest possible context for Milton's invocations. The nine psalms of which he made metrical translations in April 1648 show how deeply he understood the invocatory nature of the Psalms and their status as acts of the human voice, for the words underscored are his own conscious additions, so signalized by himself:

Wilt thou not turn, and *hear our voice*
  And us again revive. . . .

(85:6)

I lift my soul *and voice* . . .

(86:3)

I in the day of my distress
  Will call on thee *for aid*.

(86:7)[14]

The role of the human voice in the psalmody, Milton seems to have recognized, is to represent unremitting aspiration toward God's presence—a recognition he seems to stress by his application of the word; for the translating poet adds the adjective "incessant" to man's "praiers" (86:6). Because it is a vehicle of transcendence, either hoped for or realized, and a sign of man's special relation to the divine source, the human voice tends to affirm in the Psalms a certain transcendent character of its own, invested with an almost divine lyrical power and sustained by the harp's music and the singer's repetitive incantation. The voice lifting the song to heaven becomes for the Western religious imagination a powerful and enduring image, a recurrent sign of man's special place in God's creation and of his intimate relation to the all-powerful Lord.

THE MEANING, NOT THE NAME

In the Psalms, voice does not so much define as approach and envelop meaning. Through incantatory repetition and a various winnowing of image after image, the individual psalm comes to embody a meaning that it cannot name, just as the ultimate object of the singer's address is a mystery ultimately unnameable, although addressed by several names.[15]

Milton's invocations adopt a similar posture. They circle and recircle the numinous source of their power with ever varying name and image, but, as in a dance, the movement gradually assumes an order and embodies meaning before our eyes. Thus the speaker's relation to his divine source of inspiration necessarily assumes a variety of shapes. He turns from Heavenly Muse to Spirit, to Light, to Urania, in order to invoke a source that is all of these, but more. As he had once reminded his friend Diodati, "Many are the shapes of things divine."[16] Adam's first namings seem at first glance unlike Milton's —spontaneous knowings, revealing an intuition of the ideal correspondence between words and things:

> . . . to speak I tri'd, and forthwith spake,
> My Tongue obey'd and readily could name
> What e're I saw . . .
>
> (VIII.271−72)

and doubtless Milton means us to understand this as one of the abilities of the unfallen mind. Still, even Adam, rejoicing in his ability to name and know, discovers that intuitive naming fails when it attempts to go beyond created things to their uncreated source in God:

> I nam'd them, as they pass'd, and understood
> Thir Nature, with such knowledg God endu'd
> My sudden apprehension: but in these
> I found not what me thought I wanted still;
> And to the Heav'nly vision thus presum'd.
>   O by what Name, for thou above all these,
> Above mankinde, or aught then mankinde higher,
> Surpassest farr my naming, how may I
> Adore thee, Author of this Universe, . . .
>
> (VIII.352−60)

Like Adam addressing God, Milton encounters in his Muse a divine source of illumination that surpasses far his naming. Adam calls Him "Author of this Universe," just as Milton grants his Muse various traditional and even improvised titles; but both sustain their invoca-

tions with a full awareness that the names are insufficient. Either by
accident or intent Milton thus provides within the epic itself the
paradigm needed to interpret the invocations it contains, a paradigm
stressing both the transcendence of the divine otherness upon whose
help he depends and the nearness of its presence.[17]

Because the invocations explicitly acknowledge that the Muse,
like all divinity, ultimately surpasses the poet's naming, they seem
almost to rejoice in proliferating contexts for interpretation, without
interpreting decisively themselves. Nowhere is this more true than in
the invocation to light, with its dazzling profusion of biblical, theological, and philosophical allusions:

> Hail holy Light, ofspring of Heav'n first-born,
> Or of th' Eternal Coeternal beam
> May I express thee unblam'd? since God is light,
> And never but in unapproached light
> Dwelt from Eternitie, dwelt then in thee,
> Bright effluence of bright essence increate.
> Or hear'st thou rather pure Ethereal stream,
> Whose Fountain who shall tell?
>
> (III. 1 – 8)

Milton seems actually to praise the multiplicities in light's identity,
and is able to praise them "unblam'd" because he alone has had the
unnameable experience, which only his voice and his various namings
and unnamings can convey. Thus he begins in the interrogatory mood,
as Adam opens his address to God: "O by what Name . . . how may I
Adore thee."

He then recalls the priority of voice, by remembering the act of
speech that created the world:

> . . . before the Sun,
> Before the Heavens thou wert, and at the voice
> Of God, as with a Mantle didst invest
> The rising world of waters dark and deep,
> Won from the void and formless infinite . . .
>
> (III. 8 – 12)

an account that itself echoes Psalm 104:

> Who coverest thyself with light as with a garment.
>
> (Ps. 104:2)

With this recognition of both psalmist voice and creative speech, he is ready to proceed with the invocation: "Thee I re-visit now" (III.13).

Such struggles to find a language in which to "re-visit," and be visited by, transcendence have an interesting analogy in Augustine, from whose pages Milton may have drawn example as well as strength:

> Grant me (Lord) to know and understand what I ought first to doe, whether call upon thee, or praise thee? and which ought to be first, to know thee, or to call upon thee?
>
> But who can rightly call upon thee, that is yet ignorant of thee? for such an one may in stead of thee call upon another. Or art thou rather *(first)* called upon, that thou mayest so come to bee knowne? . . . And again, *They shall praise the Lord that seeke after him:* For, *They that seeke, shall finde;* and finding, they shall praise him. Thee will I seeke, O Lord, calling upon thee; and I will call upon thee believing in thee: for thou has beene declared unto us. My faith (O Lord) calls upon thee, which thou hast inspired into me; even by the humanity of thy Sonne, and by the ministery of thy Preacher.[18]

In prolonging his meditation on this crucial theme, Augustine, like Milton, remembers the Creation:

> And how shall I call upon my God, my Lord and God? because that when I invoke him, I call him into my selfe: and what place is there in me, fit for my God to come into me by, whither God may come into me; even that God which made Heaven and Earth? Is it so, my Lord God? is there any thing in me capable of thee? Nay, can both Heaven and earth which thou hast made, and in which thou hast made me, in any wise containe thee?
>
> (I.2)

As with Milton's invocations, Augustine's book returns to the Psalms for model. One third, in fact, of all biblical quotations or paraphrases in the *Confessions* are from the Psalms,[19] and the first words of the opening meditation are an invocation and quotation of the Psalms:

> Great are Thou, (O Lord) and greatly to be praised: great is thy power, yea and thy Wisedome is infinite. And man,

who being a part of what thou hast created, is desirous to
praise thee . . .

$$(I.1)^{20}$$

What is particularly interesting about all this background for
Milton is that, as so often in the later poet's work, Augustine's pro-
cedure is to make his invocations a searching meditation on the very act
of invocation they perform. The word *invocare* appears eight times in
the first section of his *Confessions*, three times in the second,[21] and in
the final book, the plea *invoco te* reverberates throughout—so much so
that his seventeenth-century translator Watts entitles this section *"He
calleth upon God."*

> I call upon thee, O my *God*, my *mercy*; upon thee that
> createdst me, and, who hast not forgotten him, that had
> forgotten thee. I invite thee into my soule, which by a
> desire that thy selfe inspireth into her, thou now preparest
> to entertayne thee. Forsake mee not now when I call upon
> *thee*, whom thou preventest before I call'd: having beene
> earnest with mee with much variety of repeated calls; that
> I would heare thee from a far, and suffer my selfe to be
> converted, and call at length upon thee, that now calledst
> after me . . .
>
> (XIII.1)

As is evident in this excerpt, Augustine's psalmist confession holds
that the direction of a man's life involves a mysterious union of two
voices: a vocation discovered through invocation of the ultimate *vox*.
This union—emphasized by his etymological play *et vocantem me
invocarem te* (XIII.1)—led in life to a conversion, or turning, which
he emphasizes in the passage above by using the verb *convertere* in the
phrase "and suffer my selfe to be converted." But the turning, of
course, was preceded by a prolonged inner conflict. As the tension
nears its climax in the narrative, quotations throng from the Psalms of
Lament, which, we remember, originally were sung "by individuals
during personal crises." If these psalms can become for Augustine
formulations of personal distress as well as prayers for aid, it is possible
that Milton's epic invocations, which depend upon their imagery,
themes, and structure, may also reflect, at some level, an experience of
crisis—and a cure.

THE UPRIGHT HEART AND PURE

From the youthful burner of midnight oil to "the Poet blind, yet bold" whom Marvell celebrated in his verses "On Paradise Lost, " Milton struggled with defining and then realizing his task as an epic poet.[22] The early choices, conflicts, setbacks, and reassertions on the road to poethood have been carefully detailed and documented.[23] His early enthusiasm for Platonic idealism is characteristic of the energy and impatience that empower the epic flight during his later phase: "Nor did Ceres, according to the fable, ever seek her daughter Proserpine with such unceasing solicitude, as I have sought this idea of the beautiful in all the forms and appearance of things (for many are the forms of the divine). I am wont day and night to continue my search . . . ."[24] Later, the poet of *Paradise Lost* will search night and day for his inspiration, for he will not be alone, he tells his Muse, when "thou / Visit'st my slumbers Nightly, or when Morn / Purples the East" (VII.28−30).

At several times during his life Milton evaluates his progress toward a vocation that can match his profound ambition; these evaluations characteristically reveal an anxiety about finding a fulfillment, calmed only by the thought of divine guidance. Compare, for example, these two famous sonnets, composed about twenty years apart:

> How soon hath time the suttle theef of youth,
>> Stoln on his wing my three and twentieth yeer!
>> My hasting dayes flie on with full career,
>> But my late spring no bud or blossom shew'th.
> Perhaps my semblance might deceive the truth,
>> That I to manhood am arriv'd so near,
>> And inward ripenes doth much less appear,
>> That som more timely-happy spirits indu'th.
> Yet be it less or more, soon or slow,
>> It shall be still in strictest measure eev'n,
>> To that same lot, however mean or high,
> Toward which Time leads me, and the will of Heav'n;
>> All is, if I have grace to use it so,
>> As ever in my great task Masters eye.
>> (Sonnet 7, 1632)

> When I consider how my light is spent,
>> E're half my days, in this dark world and wide,

And that one Talent which is death to hide,
Lodg'd with me useless, though my Soul more bent
To serve therewith my Maker, and present
My true account, least he returning chide,
Doth God exact day-labour, light deny'd,
I fondly ask; But patience to prevent
That murmur, soon replies, God doth not need
Either man's work or his own gifts, who best
Bear his milde yoak, they serve him best, his State
Is Kingly. Thousands at his bidding speed
And post o're Land and Ocean without rest:
They also serve who only stand and waite.

(Sonnet 19, 1652?)

Despite the distance of two decades especially crucial for the development of a major poet, these poems show a remarkable similarity. In both we catch a glimpse of a poet who fears he may be dangerously stalled in his progress, but who relies on the grace and wisdom of God to aid him. Both are, in essence, sketches of a moment in vocational crisis.

Although they too are well known, it is helpful in this context to remember several passages of his prose, for their tone reveals better than any commentary the stress and pressures of the choice and fulfillment of vocation:

He who would not be frustrate of his hope to write well hereafter in laudable things, ought him selfe to bee a true Poem, that is, a composition, and patterne of the best and honourablest things; not presuming to sing high praises of heroick men, or famous Cities, unless he have in himselfe the experience and the practice of all that which is praise-worthy.[25]

When, later, in "The Reason of Church Government," he reviews the grand roll call of the highest classical and biblical models for his own prospective achievement—Homer, Vergil, Tasso, the Book of Job, Sophocles, Euripides, the Song of Solomon, the Revelation of St. John, Pindar, Callimachus, and finally, the Psalms—he concludes with a passage that is one of the best apologies for poetry ever made:

These abilities [i.e., those of the Poet], wheresoever they be

found, are the inspired guift of God rarely bestow'd, but yet
to some (though most abuse) in every Nation: and are of
power beside the office of a pulpit, to imbreed and cherish in
a great people the seeds of vertu, and publick civility, to
allay the perturbations of the mind, and set the affections in
right tune, to celebrate in glorious and lofty Hymns the
throne and equipage of Gods Almightinesse, and what he
works, and what he suffers to be wrought with high
providence in his Church, to sing the victorious agonies of
Martyrs and Saints, the deeds and triumphs of just and pious
Nations doing valiantly through faith against the enemies of
Christ, to deplore the general relapses of Kingdoms and
States from justice and Gods true worship. Lastly,
whatsoever in religion is holy and sublime, in vertu
amiable, or grave, whatsoever hath passion or admiration in
all the changes of that which is call'd fortune from without,
or the wily suttleties and refluxes of man's thoughts from
within, all these things with a solid and treatable
smoothnesse to paint out and describe. Teaching over the
whole book of sanctity and vertu through all the instances of
example with such delight to those especially of soft and
delicious temper who will not so much as look upon Truth
herselfe, unlesse they see her elegantly drest, that whereas
the paths of honesty and good life appear now rugged and
difficult, though they be indeed easy and pleasant, they
would then appeare to all men both easy and pleasant though
they were rugged and difficult indeed.[26]

Thus the great poet must be prepared by God with more than
poetic greatness; almost as a function of his poethood, he must be an
examplary priest, orator, psalmist, prophet, and teacher; and with
characteristic fearlessness Milton then advances to claim his own
future fulfillment of these high expectations:

Neither doe I think it shame to covnant with any knowing
reader, that for some few yeers yet I may go on trust with
him toward the payment of what I am now indebted, as
being a work not to be rays'd from the heat of youth, or the
vapours of wine, like that which flows at wast from the pen
of some vulgar Amorist, or the trencher fury of a riming

parasite, nor to be obtain'd by the invocation of Dame
Memory and her Siren daughters, but by devout prayer to
that eternall Spirit who can enrich with all utterance and
knowledge, and sends out his Seraphim with the hallow'd
fire of his Altar to touch and purify the lips of whom he
pleases.[27]

When Milton finally paid his debt by writing *Paradise Lost*, he
was able at last, as he had promised, to make his "devout prayer to that
eternall Spirit who can enrich with all utterance and knowledge":

> And chiefly Thou O Spirit, that dost prefer
> Before all Temples th' upright heart and pure,
> Instruct me, for Thou know'st; Thou from the first
> Wast present, and with mighty wings outspread
> Dove-like satst brooding on the vast Abyss
> And mad'st it pregnant: What in me is dark
> Illumin, what is low raise and support;
> That to the highth of this great Argument
> I may assert Eternal Providence,
> And justifie the wayes of God to men.
>
> *(Paradise Lost* I.17−26)

Much of the great power of the invocations rises from the intense
hidden drama embodied in them, revealing Milton in the process of
overcoming the enduring crises of his poethood and life. Here they
differ from the Crisis Psalms which are so deeply embedded in them;
for those psalms portray the singer almost overwhelmed by crisis,
praying for the deliverance that is yet to come; whereas the invocations
of Milton show him in the process of triumph, overcoming the crisis
and securing his poem. The triumph emerges before us as the turning
of the verse unfolds.

> Of Mans First Disobedience, and the Fruit
> Of that Forbidden Tree, whose mortal tast
> Brought Death into the World, and all our woe,
> With loss of *Eden,* till one greater Man
> Restore us, and regain the blissful Seat,
> Sing Heav'nly Muse . . .
>
> *(Paradise Lost* I.1−6)

Johnson held that it was the peculiar power of Milton's verse to astonish the reader. Of no lines in *Paradise Lost* is this more true than of these opening lines, compelling the reader to attention with the expectation, as C. S. Lewis phrased it, *"That some great thing is about to begin."*[28] A recent critic has responded to Lewis: "I believe that in them the 'great thing' has already begun."[29] Both statements are right: the epic event, in all its power, indeed has begun; and the beginning is both a complete unit in itself and a promise—in Eliot's words, "an end and a beginning."

Yet for all the triumph breathing in these lines, the traces of crises remain, for the "devout prayer to that eternall Spirit" is itself a sign (predicted in *The Reason of Church Government*) that the poet's vocation is emerging from a crisis of unfulfilled promise, a crisis whose nature is pictured in his prayer:

> And chiefly Thou O Spirit, that dost prefer
> Before all Temples th' upright heart and pure,
> Instruct me, for Thou know'st . . .
>
> $(I.17-19)$

The image of "th' upright heart and pure" would have engaged an immediate and deep response in his seventeenth-century reader. The roots of the image go back—significantly—to the Psalms, as Milton's interpretive rendering of Psalm 4 in 1653 reveals:

> Yet know the Lord hath chose,
> Chose to himself a part
> The good and meek of heart
> (For whom to chuse he knows).
>
> $(13-16)^{30}$

In the psalm itself, the image of vocation is immediately followed by the image of invocation. Milton's rendering reads:

> Jehovah from on high
> Will hear my voyce what time to him I crie.
>
> $(17-18)$

The two images are also joined as Milton prays in his epic to the spirit who singles out "th' upright heart and pure"; like Augustine, he calls upon the One that calls to him.

Milton's other psalm translations of 1653 seem at first glance to anticipate the epic invocation's very phrase:

> On God is cast
> My defence, and in him lies
> In him who both just and wise
> Saves th' upright of Heart at last.
>
>   (Psalm 7:39−42)

But variations of the phrase recur throughout the Psalms: in one, "The upright shall dwell in thy presence" (140:13); in another, "the upright in heart" are persecuted by the wicked (11:2), as Milton represents himself to be in Book VII; in many, salvation is promised to those "upright in heart" (64:10, 36:10), and the psalmist rejoices in his vision of the triumph of the "upright" (49:14, 94:15): only "He that hath clean hands, and a pure heart" (24:4) shall ascend to the temple; only "He that walketh uprightly, . . . and speaketh the truth in his heart" (15:2) shall abide in the Lord's "tabernacle"; and, most significantly for the blind poet, only "Unto the upright there ariseth light in the darkness" (112:4).[31] No other book of the Bible presents so rich and suggestive a background for Milton's phrase, although Job, on which he so much brooded in his later years, comes close: "If thou wert pure and upright; Surely now he [God] would awake for thee, and make the habitation of thy righteousness prosperous" (8:6).[32]

For the Puritan reader of Milton's time, obsessed with "the Search for Evidences of Election,"[33] the "upright heart and pure" becomes decisive "evidence" of calling. The Puritan's typical, and deepest, despair is brought on by doubt of his election: "The only hope is to find the 'evidences' of salvation, and to this search the Puritan bent the best efforts of his mind, with the help of treatises, sermons, exemplary autobiographies, and the personal ministry of his preacher."[34] Like Bunyan bent over Scripture, he searched until he found a moment of security: "Then would the text cry, *Return unto me;* it would cry aloud, with a very great voice, *Return unto me,* for *I have redeemed thee.*"[35]

Richard Baxter, author of *The Saints Everlasting Rest* (1650), "the first Puritan treatise on the art of methodical meditation to appear in England, and one of the most popular Puritan books of the entire seventeenth century,"[36] gave his anxious readers a similar test and reassurance:

> Consider, a heart set upon heaven, will be one of the most
> unquestionable evidences of thy sincerity, and a clear
> discovery of a true work of saving grace upon thy

soul. . . . You are oft asking, How shall I know that I am truly sanctified? Why, here is a mark that will not deceive you, if you can truly say that you are possessed of it; Even, a heart set upon Heaven.[37]

Both this pervasive seventeenth-century theme and the biblical texts that nurtured it make us aware of a deeper meaning in Milton's prayer to one who prefers "th' upright heart and pure"; for we recognize now, in this elevated assertion as the epic begins, the poet's assurance to himself and us that his long-awaited fulfillment of vocation is at hand. The tomorrow promised by "Lycidas" has become *now*, and, the heart being upright, the singer may soar.

THE POET BLIND YET BOLD

It has been well observed that "the simultaneous pull in Milton's life between the impulse to get at his poem and finish it and the impulse to leave it until it ripened sufficiently to come by itself" must have produced emotional tension in the man to a degree we can hardly imagine today, a tension that came to a crisis when he went blind.[38] This crisis, bringing darkness and solitude, seems to have thrown the poet back increasingly on the resources of voice he had discovered in his earlier poems. Thus, even in the midst of his greatest prose (the *Second Defence*)[39] and in the very passage justifying his affliction, he seems almost naturally to turn to the resources of invocation:

> For my part, I call upon Thee, my God, who knowest my inmost mind and all my thoughts, to witness that (although I have repeatedly examined myself on this point as earnestly as I could, and have searched all the corners of my life) I am conscious of nothing, or of no deed, either recent or remote, whose wickedness could justly occasion or invite upon me this supreme misfortune.[40]

Indeed, the fierce defender begins his great work with a long acknowledgment of gratitude ("In the whole life and estate of man the first duty is to be grateful to God and mindful of his blessings, and to offer particular and solemn thanks without delay when his benefits have exceeded hope and prayer")[41] culminating in an invocation "not on behalf of one people nor yet one defendant, but rather for the entire human race against the foes of human liberty," from one who has "been aided and enriched by the favor and assistance of God":

> Accordingly, I beg the same immortal God that, just
> as . . . I lately defended deeds of supreme courage and
> justice, so . . . I may be able to defend . . . both the doers
> of those deeds and myself. . . .[42]

The entire passage has something of the air of a resounding prose rehearsal for the great defense and vindication in the epic to come,[43] for the defense of his blindness here shows already the fierce energy that will sustain his later epic flight:

> To be sure, we blind men are not the least of God's
> concerns, for the less able we are to perceive anything
> other than himself, the more mercifully and graciously
> does he deign to look upon us. Woe to him who mocks
> us, woe to him who injures us. He deserves to be cursed
> with a public malediction. Divine law and divine favor
> have rendered us not only safe from the injuries of men,
> but almost sacred, nor do these shadows around us seem
> to have been created so much by the dullness of our eyes as
> by the shade of angels' wings. And divine favor not
> infrequently is wont to lighten these shadows again, once
> made, by an inner and far more enduring light.[44]

This light first approaches the epic poet as an otherness. For in his epic encounter with *holy* light, he seems at first to come upon something "wholly other."[45] Since he ends with a prayer for inwardness—"Thou Celestial light / Shine inward"—his invocation perhaps dramatizes the very process by which the crisis of his blindness was mastered, through a progressive internalization that discovered new and—paradoxically—other resources of strength and energy. If "wisdom at one entrance" is "quite shut *out*" (III.50), the poet will ask light to "Shine *in*ward." His turning from *out* to *in* in these lines, as in the prose passages before, is a microcosm of the invocation's entire movement. His final insistence is upon an otherness turned inward to nourish identity and mission:

> . . . that *I* may see and tell
> Of things invisible to mortal sight.

From *out* to *in*, from "*thou* Celestial light" to "*I* may see and tell," the poet creates a double invocation: involving both a transcendent power and the deepest powers of assimilation within himself.[46]

The movement, however, is from vision to voice, from light to speech, from eye to tongue. The last phrase, "that I may *see* and *tell*," completes the register of senses by which the poet has balanced images of voice and vision. For each initial encounter with light provokes a question from the poet and a corresponding reference to voice:

> May I *express* thee unblam'd?
>
> (3)
>
> Or *hear'st* thou rather . . .?
>
> (7)
>
> Whose Fountain who shall *tell*?
>
> (8)

The inward eye sees, the outward voice seeks to respond. Like the "wakeful Bird" (line 38) singing "in shadiest Covert hid" (39), the voice arises out of experiential darkness, and the poet "Sings darkling" (39). The overall shift from seeing to telling reverses, with what may be significant implications of a maturer view, the climatic movement of the youthful "Il Penseroso," who imagines that "the pealing Organ" and "the full-voic'd Quire" will

> with sweetness, through mine ear
> Dissolve me into extasies,
> And bring all Heav'n before mine eyes.
>
> (164−66)

Milton no longer hopes to move from ecstasies of voice to finality of vision. The late sublime encounter with holy light instructs him in both the necessity of an experience no words can give and the need to sing of that experience. Response becomes responsibility, as he learns to transform his affliction into a mark of election.

IN THE MIDST OF ALL MINE ENEMIES THAT MARK

The third epic invocation, announcing that "Half yet remains unsung" and aware perhaps that the story of the Fall—the epic's "crisis," as Tillyard called it[47]—has been delayed like the poet's own fulfillment of his vocation, concentrates now on return, completion, and safety:

> . . . with like saftie guided down
> Return me to my native Element. . . .
>
> (VII.15 − 16)

The poet, like Urania, must *descend* to the mortal condition of men, an ominous horizon that becomes once more visible to the poet as he contemplates, at the apogee of his flight, the meanings of descent and Fall. He must enter into a recognition of death, "and all our woe." He must reawaken to his own mortality as a man, to the dread of abandonment by the Muse (as in Bellerophon's disaster), and to those mortal dangers which are close at hand during the reaction against the Cromwellian era.[48] The poet sings now

> with mortal voice, unchang'd
> To hoarce or mute, though fall'n on evil dayes,
> On evil dayes though fall'n, and evil tongues;
> In darkness, and with dangers compast round,
> And solitude; yet not alone, while thou
> Visit'st my slumbers Nightly, or when Morn
> Purples the East: still govern thou my Song,
> *Urania*, and fit audience find, though few.
>
> (VII.24 − 31)

He looks toward an audience of fellow mortals as the closure of his epic.

The psalmist's characteristic concern (bordering at times on obsession) with enemies becomes in this passage such a fully developed crisis of confrontation that at least one reader has found in it "a trace of nightmare terror."[49] It is certainly, at the least, a suspenseful meeting with a mirage of enemies, death not the least among them and, as always, wearing several masks. But, as in the previous invocations, the crisis is muted by the act of prayer, and the potential nightmare becomes an "empty dreame" (VII.39). The poet's situation again is transformed into a sign of election, for he knows, even while he laments, that the inspiration of the prophets, as well as of the psalmist's "Harp and Voice," arose when they were "fall'n on evil dayes . . . and evil tongues."

BREAKING THE HORRID SILENCE

↓ Milton surmounts the three successive crises of vocation, blindness, and enemies in the three direct appeals he makes to his Muse—a
pattern that emphasizes the dependence of each triumph on heavenly
aid. Primarily through these same passages, his own figure in the
poem achieves a dramatic strength and stature next to which those of
Satan appear parodies. Milton as speaker-poet enters his poem from the
very beginning in an agonistic relation to Satan, who supplies the
poem's rival voice. After one of Satan's most powerful utterances in
Book I ("Better to reign in Hell, then serve in Heav'n"), Milton
weaves into Beelzebub's response a description of that voice:

> So *Satan* spake, and him *Beelzebub*
> Thus answer'd. Leader of those Armies bright,
> Which but th' Omnipotent none could have foyld,
> If once they hear that voyce, thir liveliest pledge
> Of hope in fears and dangers, heard so oft
> In worst extreams, and on the perilous edge
> Of battel when it rag'd, in all assaults
> Thir surest signal, they will soon resume
> New courage and revive . . .
>
> (I.271−70)

Satan's "voice" is "in all assaults / Thir surest signal." In this sense it
is the real power behind the powers of hell: "to thir Generals Voyce
they soon obeyd / Innumerable" (I.337−38) and, when the daring
expedition to the New World is accepted by Satan as his responsibility, "they / Dreaded not more th' adventure then his voice"
(II.473−74). Fittingly, we first meet Satan "with bold words /
Breaking the horrid silence" (I.82−83). Silence-breaking is the burden of Satan and of the poet. "Both glorying to have scap't the *Stygian*
flood" (I.239) is a phrase that could apply not only to Satan and
Beelzebub after their flight to dry land, but also to Satan and the Milton
of the invocation to light, who has "Escap't the *Stygian* Pool" (III.14).
The Stygian pool, though most obviously a surrogate for death, is by
that very token interpretable as embracing also the boundless silence of
the voiceless poet, from which both Milton and Satan have to escape.
Of Satan's escape the poet says, "Then with expanded wings he stears
his flight" (I.225), while the poet himself flies with "bolder wing"
(III.13) or on "this flying Steed" (VII.17). Flight becomes the

poem's image of silence-breaking, of assertion and voice, of identity through strong exertion. Not to aspire, not to attempt, not to fly is for Satan—as Beelzebub perceived—"to sit in darkness here / Hatching vain Empires" (II.377−78), a direct parody of the creative action of that spirit who "Dove-like satst brooding on the vast Abyss / And mad'st it pregnant" (I.21−22).[50] Similarly, the poet may parody his own stated goal of "Things unattempted yet" (I.16) with the soon-to-follow "vain attempt" (I.44) of Satan and his bold compeers.

Satan's flight through Chaos is a flight through deformed images of voice: "a universal hubbub wilde / Of Stunning sounds and voices all confus'd" (II.951−52). His emergence is greeted by light at the end of Book II:

> But now at last the sacred influence
> Of light appears . . .
>
> (II.1,034−35)

Light here is the signal of the survival of voice, but at a cost. Satan's voice will never again be so magnificent and sublime. This is so because Satan's voice and its sublimity are now supplanted by Milton's own in the invocation to light, inspired by the "glimmering dawn" (line 1,037) that comes to Satan at the end of Book II. The supplanting is all the more powerful because we encounter the invocation for the very first time as a voice without introduction, without name. Not even "The Argument" prepares us for it, as "The Argument" of Book I had prepared us for the opening invocation. If we could possibly imagine a first reading of this invocation, it would not alert us to whose voice—Milton's or Satan's—would emerge until we had read and heard the triumph of the Miltonic sublime. The voice creates and establishes the poet's identity. And the poet's voice is not weakened, but rather strengthened, by the flight through Chaos; from which he emerges "with bolder wing . . ." (III.13). His triumph he rightly credits to special instruction:

> Taught by the heav'nly Muse to venture down
> The dark descent, and up to reascend,
> Though hard and rare . . .
>
> (III.19−21)

even as he hopes the education of Adam by Raphael and Michael, and of the reader by *Paradise Lost*, will aid in the renovation of mankind.

The invocation to light, opening Book III into the realm of Heaven, is structurally counterpointed in the most dramatic way by Satan's anti-invocation to "the full-blazing Sun" (IV.29) near the beginning of Book IV, after his descent to Mount Niphates. First, the poet opens Book IV with a cry for voice, to warn Adam and Eve of their imminent danger:

> O for that warning voice, which he who saw
> Th' *Apocalypse*, heard cry in Heaven aloud,
> Then when the Dragon, put to second rout,
> Came furious down to be reveng'd on men,
> *Wo to the inhabitants on Earth!* that now,
> While time was, our first-Parents had bin warnd
> The coming of thir secret foe, and scap'd
> Haply so scap'd his mortal snare; for now
> *Satan,* now first inflam'd with rage, came down,
> The Tempter ere th' Accuser of man-kind . . .
>
> (IV.1−10)

Satan soon encounters an unexpected, but temporary, reversal, the distraction of self-doubt: "And like a devillish Engine back recoiles / Upon himself" (IV.17−18). Milton prepares the way for parody by revising the famous chiasmus proposed by Satan in Book I:

> The mind is its own place, and in it self
> Can make a Heav'n of Hell, a Hell of Heav'n.
>
> (I.254−55)

For the chiastic project of the second line, Milton now substitutes the powerful revision:

> The Hell within him, for within him Hell . . .
>
> (IV.20)

The parody is appropriate because it recognizes and assaults upon its own ground one of Satan's most characteristic rhetorical modes. Milton also now counters the claim that "the mind is its own place" with

> . . . nor from Hell
> One step no more then from himself can fly
> By change of place . . .
>
> (IV.21−23)

The stage is thus set for Satan's anti-invocation to light, the parodistic parallel to Milton's earlier invocation.[51]

> O thou that with surpassing Glory crownd,
> Look'st from thy sole Dominion like the God
> Of this new World; at whose sight all the Starrs
> Hide thir diminisht heads; to thee I call,
> But with no friendly voice, and add thy name
> O Sun, to tell thee how I hate thy beams
> That bring to my remembrance from what state
> I fell . . .
>
> (IV.32−39)

The long dramatic soliloquy that begins here shows both the similarities and differences between Satanic soliloquy and Miltonic invocation. The imagery of voice is nominally present in Satan's speech ("with no friendly voice"); but Satan, here alone for the first time in the epic drama, presents a weaker version of that self he can project in dialectical discourse or before great audiences. Alone, he makes an admission of creaturehood ("me, whom he created what I was / In that bright eminence" (IV.43−44) that he fiercely denies to Abdiel:

> We know no time when we were not as now;
> Know none before us, self-begot, self-rais'd . . .
>
> (V.859−60)

Thus Milton undercuts one of Satan's strongest illusions: "none before us." In his anti-invocation Satan is content merely to name the sun—a significant contrast to Milton's invocations—because he wants to advance so quickly to an expression of his hatred. Yet that is partly the result of the dramatic situation into which Milton has inserted him and thus in itself is a reminder of Milton's creating voice.[52]

Most of all, Satan's soliloquy may be seen as a parody of Milton's invocation because it denies that transcendence of solitude is possible; its posture is doomed solipsism. As one analysis has made clear, "Satan himself undermines his stance; turning physical realms into metaphors of consciousness, he pulls the ground from under himself and makes the fall bottomless. His understanding is decreative, for all space between the cosmic poles of heaven and hell is likewise collapsed into solipsism."[53] Satan does not call for aid—like Milton—but to curse the alternative of help.

The inspiration and humility that distinguish Milton's invocation are, then, central to the overall pattern: the turning toward otherness and the prayed-for internalization of that light. Despite this poet's having suffered an isolating defeat in his blindness, as Satan's fall and "steep flight" (III.741) have isolated him, Milton alone can say:

> Yet not the more
> Cease I to wander where the Muses haunt
> Cleer Spring, or shadie Grove, or Sunnie Hill,
> Smit with the love of sacred Song . . .
>
> (III.26−29)

And where Satan's memory "of what he was, what is" (IV.25) is "bitter" (IV.24), Milton's has become poignantly long-suffering and serene:

> Thus with the Year
> Seasons return, but not to me returns
> Day, or the sweet approach of Ev'n or Morn,
> Or sight of vernal bloom, or Summers Rose,
> Or flocks, or heards, or human face divine . . .
>
> (III.40−44)[54]

For all his possible sublimity, Satan is trapped in the rhetorical universe of the poem that Milton created.[55] The ultimate privilege of voice is the author's, and that is why in a perhaps surrealistic sense we often feel that the Satan of the first two Books attempts to become the author of the poem. The invocation to light signals the emerging victory of Milton as poet over even the most powerful and sublime of his creations. The voice of the victorious poet simultaneously establishes his identity and authority. And the history of English poetry has sustained and even enlarged the dimensions of that victory.

New Amaze

> *Thus we rejoyc'd, but soon our joy is turn'd*
> *Into perplexity and new amaze . . .*
> *Paradise Regain'd*

If we were now turning from the great epic to *Paradise Regained* for the first time, we might expect from its title to be entering the paradise within promised by the epic, but we would find only a "wast Wilderness" (I.7). "Wilderness" and "wilde" are repeatedly used to describe the setting of this "brief epic" of temptation. As in Milton's first great exploration of the temptation theme in the *Mask*, the characters here are "Wandring this woody maze" (*Paradise Regained* II.246). Like Comus, Satan plots "well woven snares" (I.97) to subdue his victim. His first words to Christ—"Sir, what ill chance hath brought thee to this place . . .?" (I.321)—recall Comus's first question to the lady: "What chance good Lady hath bereft you thus?" (*Mask*, line 276). The Holy Spirit seems, in a way, to take the place of the earlier "attendant Spirit" when Christ walks forth alone, "the Spirit leading" (I.189).

Like the *Mask*, *Paradise Regained* is an exploration of the varied powers of voice, from demonic to human to divine, and a meditation on the intervening of divine voice in human history. For

God hath now sent his living Oracle
Into the World, to teach his final will,
And sends his Spirit of Truth henceforth to dwell
In pious Hearts, an inward Oracle
To all truth requisite for men to know.

(I.460−64)

To acknowledge this "inward Oracle" dwelling in the heart of his story, Milton, at the outset of the poem, invokes

Thou Spirit who ledst this glorious Eremite
Into the Desert, his Victorious Field
Against the Spiritual Foe, and broughtst him thence
By proof the undoubted Son of God, inspire,
As thou art wont, my prompted Song else mute,
And bear through highth or depth of natures bounds
With prosperous wing full summ'd to tell of deeds
Above Heroic, though in secret done,
And unrecorded left through many an Age,
Worthy t' have not remain'd so long unsung.

(I.8−17)

The poet asks the Spirit that led Christ into the desert to lead him into the song, located—it would seem—in a wilderness at the extremes of "natures bounds" (line 13), thus giving us perhaps the first clue to a

pattern of association between poet and Son of God, soon to be confirmed by our introduction to Christ, who is—like the poet—"alone,
the Spirit leading."

The poet's invocation is itself reinforced in the lines that immediately follow it by another voice:

> Now had the great Proclaimer with a voice
> More awful then the sound of Trumpet, cri'd . . .
>
> (I.18−19)

Thus Milton places his own voice as the introduction to a series of
voices; for not only does St. John's proclamation begin the story, the
ensuing account of the baptism emphasizes that

> Heaven open'd, and in likeness of a Dove
> The Spirit descended, while the Fathers voice
> From Heav'n pronounc'd him his beloved Son.
>
> (I.30−32)

"That heard the Adversary" (I.33) introduces us to Satan, who is "with
the voice divine / Nigh Thunder-struck" (I.35−36) and who then
counterpoints the poet's prayer to the Spirit with the invocatory address
that constitutes his first speech:

> O ancient Powers of Air and this wide world . . .
>
> (I.44)

Almost as if part of a meditative design, the account of the
proclamation of the Son is given three times in Book I: first, as we just
witnessed, by the poet (lines 18−32); now by Satan who tells to "th'
infernal Crew" he saw

> A perfect Dove descend, what e're it meant,
> And out of Heav'n the Sov'raign voice I heard
> This is my Son belov'd, in him am pleas'd;
>
> (I.83−85)

and finally by Christ Himself:

> The Baptist . . .
> Strait knew me, and with loudest voice proclaim'd
> Me him (for it was shew'n him so from Heaven)
> Me him whose Harbinger he was . . .
> . . . as I rose out of the laving stream,

Heaven open'd her eternal doors, from whence
The Spirit descended on me like a Dove,
And last the sum of all, my Father's voice,
Audibly heard from Heav'n, pronounc'd me his . . .
(I.270; 275—77; 280—84)

From voice of poet to speech of Satan, from the Baptist's proclamation
to God's own voice, we are introduced to a spiritual-auditory world
even more wide-ranging than the maze of sound in *Comus*, and more
engaged with the traditional forms of divine communication—a world
in which God's speech is celebrated by a heavenly harmony of voice and
music ("all Heaven / Admiring . . . into Hymns / Burst forth . . .
while the hand / Sung with the voice" (I.168—69; 171—72) and the
Nativity of the Word is greeted by "a glorious Quire / Of Angels in the
fields of Bethlehem" (I.242—43).

Amid this array of voices, the action of Book I emphasizes that
this "brief epic" begins the moment that God

Audibly heard from Heav'n, pronounc'd me his,
Me his beloved Son, in whom alone
He was well pleas'd; by which I knew the time
Now full, that I no more should live obscure,
But openly begin, as best becomes
The Authority which I deriv'd from Heaven.
And now by some strong motion I am led
Into this Wilderness . . .
(I.284—91)

Here the "plot" of Milton's story truly starts, for, by the Father's voice,
the Son knows "that I *no more should live obscure,* / *But openly begin.*"
And, as we have come to expect in Milton, the divine call to "one
greater Man" answers the age-old human invocation to God, spoken in
this poem by "Plain Fishermen" (II.27):

God of Israel,
Send thy Messiah forth, the time is come . . .
(II.42—43)

But the question remains when the solitary Christ has, like the
meditative poet, "Into himself descended," "How to begin, how to
accomplish best / His end of being on Earth" (II.111, 113—14).
What seems to absorb Milton's imagination in the drama, as it unfolds,

is the trial by which man's voice preserves what God's voice has given, how

> Man lives not by Bread only, but each Word
> Proceeding from the mouth of God . . .
>
> (I.349−50)

Indeed, the drama of *Paradise Regained* seems almost deliberately stripped of everything but voice. Satan and Christ each struggle to assert a rhetoric that will master the other. The poem moves forward as a debate between the Word and the "great Dictator" (I.113) whose "words impression left / Of much amazement to th' infernal Crew . . ." (I.106−7). But where Satan can dictate to the devils, he must return an "Answer smooth" (I.467) to the Son of God—a strategy doomed eventually to "shameful silence" (IV.22):

> The Tempter stood, nor had what to reply,
> Discover'd in his fraud, thrown from his hope,
> So oft, and the perswasive Rhetoric
> That sleek't his tongue, and won so much on Eve,
> So little here, nay lost . . .
>
> (IV.2−6)

Thus, at the end, the serpent is fittingly reprimanded from heaven:

> hereafter learn with awe
> To dread the Son of God: hee all unarm'd
> Shall chase thee with the terror of his voice . . .
>
> (IV.624−26)

Paradise Regained, because of the austerity of this focus, seems to put the vision of Paradise even further beyond its ken than *Paradise Lost* had placed it, since there at least the garden is imaged before its loss. Milton's imagination returns here to the motif of self-purification almost as if to insist again on the great truth of *Areopagitica:* "that which purifies us is triall, and triall is by what is contrary." Though his ultimate purpose is to show "the Victory and Triumph of the Son of God" (I.173), the mood is not always one of celebration (as we might expect after the poet's "Triumph" over Satan in *Paradise Lost*), but often of conflict:

> O what a multitude of thoughts at once
> Awaken'd in me swarm, while I consider

> What from within I feel my self, and hear
> What from without comes after to my ears . . .
>
> (I.196−99)

It is a drama, one is sometimes tempted to say, not of paradise regained, but of crisis renewed.[56]

The austere mood seems particularly noticeable in the Redeemer's notorious severity toward the classics (IV.328−64). Because we tend to see Christ in this poem at least partly as "Milton himself imagined perfect,"[57] it is difficult to read Christ's speech on Greek and Roman literature and philosophy as a renunciation by Milton himself. For if it is Milton speaking, he "goes out of his way to hurt the dearest and oldest inhabitants of his mind"[58] in order to exalt Hebrew literature and wisdom almost exclusively:

> All our Law and Story strew'd
> With Hymns, our Psalms with artful terms inscrib'd,
> Our Hebrew Songs and Harps . . .
>
> (IV.334−36)

But now we are in a position at least to speculate about the reasons for this high elevation of the "Psalms with artful terms inscrib'd" because we have seen the increasing role these "holy Psalms" ("At a Solemn Musick," line 15) have played in the author's poetic progress, in the images and structure of his epic invocations, and perhaps even in the recovery of inspiration that made *Paradise Lost* possible.

But now we sense, in addition, the eccentric mood of a solitary old rebel when we hear the fantastic assertion that Greece "deriv'd" (IV.338) all her poetry from the Hebrew Scripture. In a way like Joyce blindly brooding over *Finnegans Wake*, he makes the colossal error of ascribing the most immediate sources of his own inspiration to the very structure of world history. For we can only suppose that Milton in his old age found expressed in the Psalms "what for him was of all things most important, the communion of the isolated human being with God."[59]

SEPARATE TO GOD

The Christ of *Paradise Regained* begins his mission "by some strong motion . . . led / Into this Wilderness, to what intent I learn not yet, perhaps I need not know" (line 290−92), after thinking that

he had been "born" (line 205) to a simpler end of learning, excellence
and public service (201 – 14)—all Greek and Roman classical ideals
that did not prepare him for the Hebraic crisis of the wilderness.[60] The
Son's first speech, as we have seen, is a confession of this dawning
crisis, of expectations that must be revised ("Ill sorting with my present
state," line 200): "O what a multitude of thoughts at once / Awaken'd
in me swarm."

Samson Agonistes opens with its hero experiencing a strikingly
similar crisis, led by a "guiding hand" and seeking ease

> From restless thoughts, that like a deadly swarm
> Of Hornets arm'd, no sooner found alone,
> But rush upon me thronging and present
> Times past, what once I was, and what am now.
>
> (19 – 22)

Like the Christ who remembers the signs of election at his Nativity,
Samson asks

> O wherefore was my birth from Heaven foretold
> Twice by an Angel . . . ?
>
> (23 – 24)

His opening meditation pursues this theme with insistent vigor, as we
glimpse the true inward dimensions of his "Agon":

> Why was my breeding order'd and prescrib'd
> As of a person separate to God,
> Design'd for great exploits; if I must dye
> Betray'd, Captiv'd, and both my Eyes put out,
> Made of my Enemies the scorn and gaze;
> To grind in Brazen Fetters under task
> With this Heav'n-gifted strength?
>
> (30 – 36)

Election, blindness, enemies: the three great crises of the invoking poet of Paradise Lost are now to be given the embodiment "Of that
sort of Dramatic Poem which is call'd Tragedy."[61] Much as the Book
of Job portrays in dramatic form the structure, themes, and images of
crisis in the Psalms, the poet of Paradise Lost now will entrust the
culminating crises of his life and poethood to that form "said by
Aristotle to be of power by raising pity and fear, or terror, to purge the

mind of those and such like passions."[62] That Milton's preface to *Samson* should leap first to the power discussed last in the *Poetics*— catharsis—suggests that we may be close to the heart of his design. To "purge the mind" reformulates his earlier request that light may "purge and disperse" the mists of doubt and ignorance dividing him, then as now, from "calm of mind all passion spent."[63]

In this poem, the characters will make the poet's psalmist pleas for him:

> God of our Fathers, what is man!
> That thou towards him with hand so various . . .
>
> (667−68)

The hero will recognize his responsibility: "Sole Author I, sole cause . . ." (line 376); the plot will be a story of continuous inspiration, of

> Secret refreshings, that repair his strength,
> And fainting spirits uphold . . .
>
> (665−66)

a story whose very action will turn on "Some rousing motions," as Samson puts it, "which dispose / To something extraordinary my thoughts. / I with this Messenger will go along" (lines 1,382−84). The chorus's single comment on this speech—"In time thou hast resolv'd, the man returns" (line 1,390)—confirms that we have indeed reached a "turning point," where the unexpected discovery of calling will be succeeded by Samson's recovery of his mission as deliverer—a drama of vocation regained.

In this sense, Milton's tragedy, like his "brief epic," has its roots in his early *Mask*. There we saw that the threat to "insnared chastity" might possibly be an objectification of the threat to vocation. If so, *Samson Agonistes* relives this attack in a strangely heightened fashion, reminiscent of the psalmist's complaint of being "ensnared" by enemies.[64] For Samson is an "Ensnar'd" (line 365) hero whose "faithless enemy" (380)—Dalila—is his "accomplisht snare" (230). His fall is his failure to shake off "all her snares" (line 409): "swoll'n with pride into the snare I fell / Of fair fallacious looks" (532−33). When he confronts her face to face, he promises never "To bring my feet again into the snare / where once I have been caught" (931−32).

Yet, in a sense, the hero dies an "ensnared" death—entrapped by

the crumbling "Theatre" (line 1,605) he has pulled down around him,
like a wounded animal that rebounds upon its hunter as it dies:

> Because they shall not trail me through thir streets
> Like a wild Beast, I am content to go.
>
> (1,402−3)

The tragedy thus captures man's darkest animal nature at the very
moment of triumph that illuminates his divine possibility. For of his
god-like triumph the semichorus sings:

> as an Eagle
> His cloudless thunder bolted on thir heads . . .
>
> (1,695−96)

twice crediting his victory to transcendent "vertue" (meaning both
power and fidelity):

> So vertue giv'n for lost,
> Deprest, and overthrown, as seem'd,
> Like that self-begott'n bird
> In the Arabian woods embost,
> That no second knows nor third,
> And lay e're while a Holocaust,
> From out her ashie womb now teem'd,
> Revives, reflourishes, then vigorous most
> When most unactive deem'd,
> And though her body die, her fame survives,
> A secular bird ages of lives.
>
> (1,697−1,707)

If "vertue" seems to survive and even grow in power through Milton's
poetry, ultimately representing an intimate sense of vocation, the
Semichorus's celebration sums up in one song the hero's triumph over
the crises of vocation, blindness, and enemies that plagued him in his
opening soliloquy. For

> he thow blind of sight,
> Despis'd and thought extinguish't quite,
> With inward eyes illuminated
> His fierie vertue rouz'd
> From under ashes into sudden flame . . .
>
> (1,687−91)

Yet, in keeping with the prevailing mood of this "Tragedy," the motive for invocation is most often expressed, as in Samson's first words, in apostrophes of lamentation:

> O loss of sight, of thee I most complain!
>
> (67)

> O dark, dark, dark, amid the blaze of noon . . .
>
> (80)

> O first created Beam, and thou great Word,
> Let there be light, and light was over all;
> Why am I thus bereav'd thy prime decree?[65]
>
> (83—85)

This mood of lamentation spreads to the other characters, but chiefly to Manoa:

> O miserable change! is this the man . . .   (340)

> O lastly over-strong against thy self![66]
>
> (1,590)

Manoa urges Samson to renew "praiers and vows" (line 520) to God, but the hero replies:

> His pardon I implore; but as for life,
> To what end should I seek it?
>
> (521—22)

Only "death" is "oft-invocated" (line 575) by Samson:

> This one prayer yet remains, might I be heard,
> No long petition, speedy death,
> The close of all my miseries, and the balm.
>
> (649—51)

If *Samson* is Milton's last work, it seems here almost conscious of the end of a long trial in the art of invocation. It forms, at any rate, a fitting elegy and "close" for the pattern, since only "one prayer yet remains."

The drama thus focuses on invocation in its highest and most honored form: the act of prayer. When challenged by the brute Harapha, who charges that Samson's strength is obtained by "some Magicians Art" (line 1,133), the hero presents a spirited defense of religious invocation:

> I know no Spells, use no forbidden Arts;
> My trust is in the living God . . .
> For proof hereof, if *Dagon* be thy god,
> Go to his Temple, invocate his aid
> With solemnest devotion, spread before him
> How highly it concerns his glory now
> To frustrate and dissolve these Magic spells,
> Which I to be the power of *Israel's* God
> Avow, and challenge *Dagon* to the test,
> Offering to combat thee his Champion bold,
> With th' utmost of his Godhead seconded:
> Then thou shalt see, or rather to thy sorrow
> Soon feel, whose God is strongest, thine or mine.
>
> (1,139−40, 1,145−55)

Because of his faith in a God "Whose ear is ever open" (line 1,172), Samson does not accept defeat under any circumstances. The power that ultimately redirects the hero is all the more striking for this affirmation, since the turning point in Samson's crisis is the miracle of prevenient grace: "some rouzing motions in me" (line 1,382). Perhaps it is Samson's "new acquist / Of true experience" (lines 1,755−56) in this episode that, in the words of Augustine's final recognition in the *Confessions,* "thou preventest before I call'd" (XIII.11).

Yet the final moment of apocalyptic triumph returns Milton's hero to the attitude of invocation:

> And eyes fast fixt he stood, as one who pray'd . . .
>
> (1,637)

If this is his response to the jeering mob that has just "with a shout / Rifted the air clamouring thir god with praise" (lines 1,620−21), then Samson does get his invocation contest, after all—"Ith' mid'st of all mine enemies that mark." The lamentation that resounds throughout this tragedy is fittingly ended as Samson

> At last with head erect thus cryed aloud . . .
>
> (1,640)

Once that cry has faded and the "burst of thunder" (line 1,651) with which the "Theatre" falls has died, all returns to "the sacred trust of silence" (line 428):

Nothing is here for tears, nothing to wail
Or knock the breast, no weakness, no contempt,
Dispraise or blame, nothing but well and fair,
And what may quiet us in a death so noble.

(1,721−24)

SOLE AUTHOR I

From the "secret altar" of Milton's first invocation in the Nativity Ode to the "secret top" of the passages in *Paradise Lost*—even to his meditation in *Paradise Regained* on high deeds "though in secret done" (I.15)—the poet emphasizes the "separate" and transcendent occasions of his inspiration. Finally, in *Samson*, a drama of "secret refreshings" (line 665), the hero must recover God's "holy secret" (line 496) and his own:[67]

O that torment should not be confin'd
To the bodies wounds and sores
With maladies innumerable
In heart, head, breast, and reins;
But must secret passage find
To th' inmost mind,
There exercise all his fierce accidents,
And on her purest spirits prey . . .

(606−13)

The trial of Milton's life as a poet, one is tempted to conclude, is that voice and crisis both found "secret passage" to his "inmost mind." And, as the Greek root of *crisis* seems to suggest,[68] the burdens of this situation were not only the *decisions* that were his poems (where, as in the Nativity Ode and "Lycidas," the text often "decides" the life), but also the *separations* that he endured as a man: his vocation, "separate to God" (*Samson,* line 31), his blindness, "from the chearful wayes of men / Cut off" (*Paradise Lost* III.46−47), and his enemies, "In darkness and with dangers compast round" (VII.27). Even the *secret* places of his inspiration were "separate," though transcendent. For to be "separate to God" is to risk, as Samson risks, being separated from Him: "And God not parted from him, as was feard" (*Samson,* line 1,719).

Like that "self-begott'n bird . . . That no second knows nor third" (lines 1,699 – 1,701), or the God of *Paradise Lost* — "Author of this Universe" (VIII.360)—

> Who am alone
> From all Eternity, for none I know
> Second to me or like, equal much less—
>
> (VIII.405 – 7)

the poet is a creator upon his own abyss, as indeed the repeated accounts of Creation in the epic invocations seem to insist. Like a lonely creator of worlds, Milton scatters his self-images throughout his poems—the "uncouth Swain"; Adam, Satan, and epic poet; Christ; and Samson. His early declaration that a poet "ought him selfe to bee a true Poem" finds prophetic fulfillment in the metamorphosis that seems to occur in the composition of his poems: life and art, vocation and invocation, merge—and the poet and the poem are one.

Yet out of all this creative desolation comes a voice whose one insistent message is victory. From the Ode's announcement of a New Order, to the pastoral vision of "large recompense" and "Pastures new," to the epic poet's breaking of long silence and deepening crises and even the voice of his most sublime invention, we hear that message again and again—confirmed and at last exhausted by Samson's final cry. It is almost as if the Pindaric Odes over which Milton brooded in the weeks before composing his Nativity Ode had taught his voice that the one theme worthy of Song is Victory.

Notes

1. INTRODUCTION: THE DIMENSIONS OF INVOCATION

1. All three tasks are required by the Theocritan shepherd who sings the Lament for Daphnis; he asks the Muses to "begin," "renew," and "cease the pastoral song" (*Idyll* I).

The translation of Pindar is by Richmond Lattimore, in *The Odes of Pindar* (Chicago: University of Chicago Press, 1947).

At the beginning of his *Theogony*, Hesiod's passage on the Muses—itself an invocation—gives what eventually became the accepted account of the Muses' lineage as daughters of Memory and Zeus. "Sicilian Muses," however, are invoked in Vergil's pastoral poetry because of their geographical association with Theocritus's *Idylls*, the foundation of pastoral poetry.

2. The translations of the *Georgics* and *The Art of Love* are from the Loeb editions of those works: *Virgil*, trans. H. R. Fairclough, rev. ed. (Cambridge, Mass.: Harvard University Press, 1967), I; *Ovid: The Art of Love, and Other Poems*, trans. J. H. Mozley, rev. ed. (Cambridge, Mass.: Harvard University Press, 1939).

Ovid mocks Hesiod's claim (in the *Theogony*) to have been visited by the Muses while he tended his flocks.

I draw upon Ernst Robert Curtius's detailed study of ancient, medieval, and Renaissance attitudes toward the Muses, in *European Literature and the Latin Middle Ages*, trans. Willard R. Trask, Bollingen Series XXXVI (New York: Pantheon Books, 1953), pp. 228−46.

3. But each of us must call Messalla's health over

each cupful,

And individual voices sound his absent name.

Messalla, on everyone's lips for your Aquitanian triumph,

And in your victory shedding lustre on your bearded sires,

> Draw near and inspire me with your breath, while in these
>   verses
> Due thanks is paid to the heavenly tillers of the soil.
>   (II.i.31−36)

From *The Poems of Tibullus,* trans. Philip Dunlop (Baltimore: Penguin, 1972). Michael C. J. Putnam comments: "Messalla is given the further compliment of serving as the poet's Muse. . . . In this instance the 'muse' is both alive and personally beloved," in *Tibullus: A Commentary* (Norman, Okla.: University of Oklahoma Press, 1973), p. 156.

    4. See, for example, Pindar, "Olympia" 4; and Vergil, *Georgics* I.5−23.

    5. From *Ovid's Metamorphosis: Englished, Mythologized, and Represented in Figures by George Sandys,* eds. K. K. Hulley and S. T. Vandersall (Lincoln: University of Nebraska Press, 1970).

    6. Paul de Man, "Symbolic Landscape in Wordsworth and Yeats," in *In Defense of Reading: A Reader's Approach to Literary Criticism,* eds. Reuben A. Brower and Richard Poirier (New York: Dutton, 1962), p. 22.

    7. Hesiod, *Theogony,* lines 39−40. In lines 1−115, the Muses "utter their song with lovely voice" (elsewhere in the passage, with "immortal voice," "lily-like voice," and "consenting voice"); they are "ready-voiced daughters" who appear to Hesiod and tell him "we know how to speak . . ." (trans. H. G. Evelyn-White, Loeb Classical Series, rev. ed. [London: Heinemann, 1936]). Hesiod's authority as a poet is that they "breathed into me their divine voice" (trans. Norman O. Brown, The Library of Liberal Arts [Indianapolis: Bobbs-Merrill, 1953]).

    Pindar claims "the sweet-voiced Muses shall hear me speak" ("Olympia" 6). He begins one of his odes with a lyrical invocation that movingly describes a young poet's waiting for inspiration as an expectation of the Muse's voice:

> Lady and Muse, our mother, I entreat you,
> in the holy Nemean month, come to the city thronged
>   with strangers,
> the Dorian island, Aigina; for beside
> the waters of Asopos the craftsmen of lovely
> choral songs, the young men, await your voice.
>   ("Nemea" 3)

Theocritus invokes the "clear-voiced Muses" (*Idyll* XXII) and claims himself to be "a clear voice of the Muses" (*Idyll* VII).

    8. Aristotle, *On Interpretation* (16a), trans. E. M. Edjhill, in *The Works of Aristotle, I,* Great Books of the Western World, ed. R. M. Hutchins, vol. 8 (Chicago: Encyclopaedia Britannica, 1952).

9. Plato, *Phaedrus* (274—75; 275), trans. B. Jowett, in *The Dialogues of Plato*, Great Books, vol. 7.

10. See Eric A. Havelock, *Preface to Plato* (Cambridge, Mass.: Harvard University Press, 1963).

11. See Walter J. Ong, S.J., *The Presence of the Word: Some Prolegomena for Cultural and Religious History* (New Haven: Yale University Press, 1967).

12. See Curtius, *European Literature*, pp. 234—35.

13. For a discussion of early Christian forms of invocation, see A. J. Maclean, "Invocation (Liturgical)," *Encyclopaedia of Religion and Ethics*, ed. James Hastings, 1915, VII, 407—13, esp. p. 411. The initial Christian rejection of the Muses is discussed by Curtius, *European Literature*, p. 235.

14. "The origin of prayer is to be found—essentially and existentially—in the recognition and invocation of the creator-god, the god of heaven." Rev. Adalbert G. Hamman, "Prayer," *Encyclopaedia Britannica*, 15th ed., 1974, XIV, 949.

15. "The great bulk of the hymns of the Rigveda consist of *invocations* of various deities." A. A. Macdonell, "Hymns (Vedic)," *Encyclopaedia of Religion and Ethics*, ed. James Hastings, VII, 52.

Even the later prose commentary of the *Upanishads* may shift into the invocatory mode, as in the great hymn that ends the Svetasvatara *Upanishad*.

16. Hamman, "Prayer," p. 951.

17. Jane Ellen Harrison, *Themis: A Study of the Social Origins of Greek Religion* (Cambridge: Cambridge University Press, 1912), p. 10.

In the early Greek "Hymn of Invocation," the "god invoked is not present, not there in a temple ready waiting to be worshipped; he is bidden to come, and apparently his coming, and as we shall later see his very existence, depends on the ritual that invokes him . . . All this as will later appear lands us in a region rather of magic than religion" (p. 10).

18. G. Wissowa, "Invocation (Roman)," *Encyclopaedia of Religion and Ethics*, ed. James Hastings, VII, 413.

19. A. A. Macdonell, "Hymns (Vedic)," *Encyclopaedia of Religion and Ethics*, ed. James Hastings, VII, 50.

20. For examples, see Mircea Eliade, ed., *From Primitives to Zen: A Thematic Sourcebook of the History of Religions* (New York: Harper and Row, 1967), pp. 268—86.

21. Mircea Eliade, *Shamanism: Archaic Techniques of Ecstasy*, trans. Willard R. Trask, Bollingen Series LXXVI (Princeton: Princeton University Press, 1964), p. 510.

22. Eliade, *Shamanism*, p. 510.

23. See Eliade, *Shamanism*, pp. 190 ff.

24. Eliade, *Shamanism*, p. 194.

25. Eliade, *Shamanism*, pp. 196—97.

26. Eliade concludes his study of shamanism with the speculation: "Probably a large number of epic 'subjects' or motifs, as well as many characters, images, and clichés of epic literature, are, finally, of ecstatic origin, in the sense that they were borrowed from the narratives of shamans describing their journeys and adventures in the superhuman worlds" (p. 510).

27. Like St. Bernard's prayer in the final recess of paradise, Milton's invocation to light might be described as the lyrical expression of prayer at the verge of its transfiguration into mystical experience.

See Edmund G. Gardner, *Dante and the Mystics: A Study of the Mystical Aspect of the Divina Commedia and Its Relations with Some of Its Medieval Sources* (London: Dent, 1913); and Don Cameron Allen, *The Harmonious Vision: Studies in Milton's Poetry*, rev. ed. (Baltimore: The Johns Hopkins Press, 1970), pp. 122—42.

28. Mircea Eliade, *Myths, Dreams and Mysteries: The Encounter between Contemporary Faiths and Archaic Realities*, trans. Philip Mairet, Harper Torchbooks (New York: Harper and Row, 1967), p. 36.

29. See Eliade, *Myths*, pp. 61—72.

30. See A. J. Maclean, "Invocation (Liturgical)," Hasting's *Encyclopaedia*, VII, 407—13.

31. See "Invocation," 1b, *Oxford English Dictionary*.

32. See Robert Burns Shaw, "The Call of God: The Theme of Vocation in Donne, Herbert, and Milton," Diss. Yale, December 1974.

2. THE PATTERN OF INVOCATION IN MILTON'S POETRY

1. See George deF. Lord, "Milton's Dialogue with Omniscience," *The Author in His Work: Essays on a Problem in Criticism*, ed. Louis L. Martz and Aubrey Williams (New Haven: Yale University Press, 1978).

2. For another view of the relation between Dante's and Milton's invocations, see Irene Samuel, *Dante and Milton: The Commedia and Paradise Lost* (Ithaca, N.Y.: Cornell University Press, 1966), pp. 49—66, 292—93.

3. Isabel Gamble MacCaffrey, ed., introduction, *John Milton: Samson Agonistes and the Shorter Poems*, The Signet Classical Poetry Series (New York: The New American Library, 1966), p. xiv.

4. *Infant* and *prophet* ultimately share the same Greek root *(phanai)*, "to speak."

5. Other minor poems that present interesting variations of the invocation pattern are "At a Vacation Exercise in the Colledge" ("Hail native Language . . ."), "Song. On May Morning" ("Hail bounteous May that dost inspire . . ."), "Upon the Circumcision" ("Ye flaming Powers . . ."), "To

Mr. H. Lawes, *on his Aires*" (where the great musician is credited with Muse-like powers of influence) and "*On the late Massacher in* Piedmont" ("Avenge O Lord thy slaughter'd Saints . . .").

6. On this possibility, see also Cleanth Brooks and J. E. Hardy, eds., *Poems of Mr. John Milton: The 1645 Edition with Essays in Analysis* (New York: Harcourt, Brace, 1951): "Milton's tribute to him becomes therefore a kind of invocation to a minor deity" (p. 126).

7. Brooks and Hardy, p. 118.

8. John Hollander notes: "It is just this union of "Voice, and Vers,'" heralded at the beginning of the poem, which some studies tend to lose sight of." I draw upon his brilliant treatment of the poem in *The Untuning of the Sky: Ideas of Music in English Poetry, 1500—1700* (Princeton: Princeton University Press, 1961), pp. 324—31.

9. Hollander, p. 331.

10. This motif may be continued in the epic invocations, if John T. Shawcross is right when he suggests that there are "sexual overtones" in Milton's portrayal of inspiration in *Paradise Lost*, drawing upon such passages as those describing the Spirit's impregnation of the world ("Dove-like satst brooding on the vast Abyss / And mad'st it pregnant," I.21—22) and the Muse's nightly visitations (VII.28—30; IX. 21—24). See "The Metaphor of Inspiration in *Paradise Lost*," in *Th' Upright Heart and Pure: Essays on John Milton Commemorating the Tercentenary of the Publication of Paradise Lost*, ed. Amadeus P. Fiore, O.F.M., Duquesne Studies: Philological Series X (Pittsburgh: Duquesne University Press, 1967), pp. 75—83.

To the extent that Milton has a classical precedent for this motif, it would, of course, be Ovid's "wanton" and "playful" Muse (*Remedia Amoris*, 362, 387).

11. See the brief but suggestive discussion of sound imagery by Kester Svendsen, "Milton's *L'Allegro* and *Il Penseroso*," *The Explicator*, 8, No. 49, (1950).

12. See Hollander, *The Untuning of the Sky*, pp. 319—22.

13. See Ernest Sirluck, "Milton's Idle Right Hand," *Journal of English and Germanic Philology*, 60 (1961), 749—85.

14. Angus Fletcher, *The Transcendental Masque: An Essay on Milton's Comus* (Ithaca, N.Y., and London: Cornell University Press, 1971), p. 166.

15. See John S. Coolidge, "Great Things and Small: The Virgilian Progression," *Comparative Literature*, 17 (1965), 1—23.

16. Brooks and Hardy, *Poems of Mr. John Milton*, p. 173.

17. *The Burning Oracle: Studies in the Poetry of Action* (London: Oxford University Press, 1939), p. 70.

18. Leslie Brisman, *Milton's Poetry of Choice and Its Romantic Heirs* (Ithaca, N.Y., and London: Cornell University Press, 1973), p. 14.

19. See Caroline W. Mayerson, "The Orpheus Image in *Lycidas*,"

PMLA, 64 (1949), 189—207.

20. Louis L. Martz explores "the growth toward maturity that constitutes this volume's dominant theme" in an essay examining closely the arrangement of the 1645 Edition: "The Rising Poet, 1645," in *The Lyric and Dramatic Milton,* English Institute Essays, ed. Joseph H. Summers (New York: Columbia University Press, 1965), pp. 3—33.

21. Prologue, Book II, "Reason of Church Government" (1642), Yale Edition, I, 820.

22. Sirluck, "Milton's Idle Right Hand," p. 750.

3.   PARADISE LOST

1. *Lives of the English Poets,* ed. George Birkbeck Hill, 3 vols. (Oxford: Clarendon Press, 1905), I, 175.

2. *Milton* (London: Chatto and Windus, 1930), p. 243. Tillyard's account (pp. 243—56) of their precise relevance to what he calls "the construction of *Paradise Lost*" is still the best commentary on this structural aspect.

For a comprehensive review of twentieth-century criticism (up to 1964) of the invocations, see Merritt Y. Hughes, "Milton and the Symbol of Light," *Studies in English Literature 1500—1900,* IV (1964), 1—33; rpt. in his *Ten Perspectives on Milton* (New Haven: Yale University Press, 1965), pp. 63—103.

Despite Tillyard's pioneering emphasis on structural significance, the main theme of subsequent research has been the identity of Milton's Muse. Readers have brought many mythological and theological backgrounds to bear on the identity of those various presences that Milton calls "Heav'nly Muse," "Spirit," "holy Light," and "Urania"—usually hoping to show that they constitute a single unity. But the labor has been, as Hughes's study reveals, inconclusive. Our look at the earlier poetry, however, seems to suggest an alternative approach to this question. From the Nativity Ode to "Lycidas," Milton prefers the role of invoker-participant adopted by the poet of *Paradise Lost,* and his early pattern of invocation appears to evolve toward a multiplicity of invocations and of presences invoked. Thus the "Swain" of "Lycidas" begins with epic sweep by invoking the Heliconian "Sisters of the sacred well, / That from beneath the seat of Jove doth spring" (and then referring to the epic Muse Calliope), but sustains his song by successive appeals to the Sicilian pastoral Muses "Arethuse" and "Alpheus." If there is, in the final analysis, an inconsistency in Milton's practice, at least it is deeply ingrained; in some respects, it even dramatizes the poet's continuing search for inspiration.

3. The best of these studies, to my mind, are Anne Davidson Ferry,

Milton's Epic Voice: The Narrator in Paradise Lost (Cambridge, Mass.: Harvard University Press, 1963); Louis L. Martz, *The Paradise Within: Studies in Vaughan, Traherne, and Milton* (New Haven: Yale University Press, 1964), pp. 105–67; and William G. Riggs, *The Christian Poet in Paradise Lost* (Berkeley: University of California Press, 1972). To their insights I most often turn when contemplating Milton's figure as narrator in his epic.

4. Rodney Delasanta, *The Epic Voice* (The Hague: Mouton, 1967), p. 14. William Kerrigan's *The Prophetic Milton* (Charlottesville: University Press of Virginia, 1974) places its central emphasis on Milton's claim to prophetic inspiration, treating the epic invocations in this context on pp. 126–43.

5. Thomas Greene, *The Descent from Heaven: A Study in Epic Continuity* (New Haven: Yale University Press, 1963), p. 3. The imaginative richness of the Christian religion, concludes Hallett Smith, was one of the reasons for Milton's success: "He found answerable style to his great argument, not only because he believed the argument, but also because he had found an area of belief which encompassed at once serious doctrine and poetic fiction." "No Middle Flight," *Huntington Library Quarterly*, 15 (1951–52), 171.

6. Galbraith Miller Crump, *The Mystical Design of Paradise Lost* (Lewisburg, Pa.: Bucknell University Press, 1975), p. 184.

7. See Greene, *The Descent from Heaven*, pp. 14–15.

8. Torquato Tasso, *Discourses on the Heroic Poem*, trans. Mariella Calvalchini and Irene Samuel (New York: Oxford University Press, 1973) p. 17.

9. This is Tasso's statement (p. 113) of Castelvetro's view, based on Castelvetro's "Opinion on the Help Poets Ask of the Muses." See the translators' note (no. 1), p. 112.

The first pages of Tasso's fourth book of the *Discourses* (pp. 111–17) deal with the subject of epic invocations, and surprisingly their special relevance to Milton's invocations has never before, to my knowledge, been studied—even in F. T. Prince's *The Italian Element in Milton's Verse* (Oxford: Clarendon Press, 1954), which says of the *Discourses* that "Milton could have found nowhere else so sustained a discussion and defence of the style he was to make his own" (p. 42).

10. Tasso, *Discourses*, p. 113.

11. *Of Education;* Yale Edition, II, 366–67.

12. Education both in the Renaissance sense referring to the moral functions of literature and in the sense recently put forward by Stanley Fish in *Surprised by Sin: The Reader in Paradise Lost* (London: Macmillan, 1967). In discussing the epic's sense of place, Tillyard emphasized that "the location of the reader is of the highest moment for understanding the construction of the

poem, for the centre of importance will be where the reader imagines himself to be situated, and not necessarily where the action is taking place" (*Milton*, pp. 245–46). The invocations, of course, as Tillyard pointed out, have special powers to create the author's (and thus the reader's) sense of place.

13. *De Trinitate*, 14.20; in *Later Works*, trans. John Burnaby, Library of Christian Classics, 8 (London: SCM Press, 1955). Quoted and discussed by Louis L. Martz, *The Paradise Within*, pp. xviii–xix. See Martz's preface, pp. xiii–xix, concerning the "Augustinian concept of interior 'illumination'."

14. Crump, *The Mystical Design*, p. 35.

15. Riggs, *The Christian Poet*, p. 37.

16. The grand opening of *Paradise Lost* naturally has elicited many critical appreciations. The most sensitive commentary of recent vintage is, in my opinion, Dame Helen Gardner's *A Reading of Paradise Lost* (Oxford: Clarendon Press, 1965), pp. 16–20. The best analyses of the exordium's powerful stylistic effects seem to me to be those of David Daiches, "The Opening of *Paradise Lost*," in *The Living Milton*, ed. Frank Kermode (London: Routledge, 1960), pp. 55–69; and Joseph H. Summers, *The Muse's Method: An Introduction to Paradise Lost* (London: Chatto and Windus, 1962), Ch. I. Davis P. Harding has shown Milton's innovative use of classical precedents in *The Club of Hercules: Studies in the Classical Background of Paradise Lost*, Illinois Studies in Language and Literature, 50 (Urbana: University of Illinois Press, 1962) 24–39.

17. The allusion was first studied by Jackson I. Cope in "Milton's Muse in *Paradise Lost*," *Modern Philology*, 55 (1957–58), 6–10 (an expanded version of which appears in his chapter on Milton's Muse in *The Metaphoric Structure of Paradise Lost* [Baltimore: The Johns Hopkins Press, 1962], pp. 149–76). Some critics have doubted whether Milton intended it; see, for example, George W. Whiting and Ann Gossman, "Siloa's Brook, the Pool of Siloam, and Milton's Muse," *Studies in Philology*, 58 (1961), 193–205.

18. See Ferry, *Milton's Epic Voice*, pp. 20–43.

19. The beginning of this prologue, like the end, assumes a listening Muse without appealing directly to her. The entire passage therefore is not an invocation in the traditional epic sense. Yet it is something very close to that. It is a raising of the poet's voice, breaking out of the epic sequence of action, introducing the subject and theme of the action to follow, and even asking for the inspiration of the Muse, but in an indirect way; for the poet expresses a *conditional* hope, "If answerable style I can obtaine / Of my Celestial Patronness" (lines 20–21), a hope that the Muse overhears and fulfills when she "deignes / Her nightly visitation unimplor'd"(lines 21–22). The prologue chooses to emphasize the prayer answered, where invocation chooses to highlight the act of prayer itself. The passage is, like the three invocations

proper, an intensely personal emergence of the poet; and, like them, it marks an important transition in the epic story. "I now must change / Those Notes to Tragic" (lines 5—6). If I discuss that passage as an invocation, it is because by now we have learned to recognize that Milton's variation on the strict form of invocation is itself one of his characteristic uses of the form.

20. "The character of Satan," says Tillyard (*Milton,* p. 277), "expresses, as no other character or act or feature of the poem does, something in which Milton believed very strongly: heroic energy." Tillyard also finds this "heroic energy" expressed in the sublimity of Milton's verse and—we might add—in the singer's ceaseless flight as depicted in the invocations.

21. Isabel Gamble MacCaffrey, *Paradise Lost as "Myth"* (Cambridge, Mass.: Harvard University Press, 1959), pp. 56, 64. The pioneering volume on Milton's poetic texture was W. B. C. Watkins's *Anatomy of Milton's Verse* (Baton Rouge: Louisiana State University Press, 1955).

22. The prologue to Book IX returns to the epic's opening in subject matter as well, by reminding us "that Man's disobedience is the main theme" (Tillyard, *Milton,* p. 253):

> I now must change
> Those Notes to Tragic; foul distrust, and breach
> And disobedience . . .
> That brought into this World a world of woe . . .
>
> (IX. 5—8, 11)

The last line, as Tillyard points out (pp. 253—54), echoes the third line of the opening: "Brought Death into the World, and all our woe."

23. Martz, *The Paradise Within,* pp. 105, 106.

24. See Ferry, *Milton's Epic Voice,* pp. 28—34.

25. Riggs, *The Christian Poet,* p. 73.

4. VOICE AND CRISIS

1. "At the close of the great morning-psalm in Paradise, the individual voice of the bard seems to join the voices of Adam and Eve," observes Martz in *The Paradise Within,* p. 109.

The avowal ("Witness if I be silent . . .") is typical of the psalmist: "If I do not remember thee, let my tongue cleave to the roof of my mouth" (Ps. 137:6).

2. Through the awakening voices of Adam and Eve, and through his own memory and art, Milton here again creates a personal "psalm," as he had done in "At a Solemn Musick," and in it, according to Hanford, "more than in any attempt to reduce the Psalms to meter, does he approach their spirit, as he elaborates with his own imagery and in his own majestic idiom the great

theme 'The Heavens declare the glory of God' " (p. 8). James Holly Hanford, "The Youth of Milton: An Interpretation of His Early Literary Development," first published in the University of Michigan *Studies in Shakespeare, Milton and Donne* (New York: Macmillan, 1925), pp. 89−163; rpt. in his *John Milton: Poet and Humanist* (Cleveland: The Press of Western Reserve University, 1966), pp. 1−74.

3. See the famous prologue to Book II of "The Reason of Church Government," Yale Edition, I, 801−23.

Martz has emphasized that the "history of English religious poetry in the sixteenth and seventeenth centuries can never be accurately recorded without remembering that for the devout poet of the time the greatest examples of religious poetry lay in the Bible." *The Poetry of Meditation: A Study in English Religious Literature of the Seventeenth Century* (New Haven: Yale University Press, 1954), p. 279.

4. A comprehensive study of this context has never before, to my knowledge, been attempted. Thus the critical comments quoted in this chapter are taken from studies with a quite different end in view.

Some readers have noticed verbal reminiscences of the Psalms in the invocations. See, for example, David Daiches, "The Opening of *Paradise Lost,*" in *The Living Milton,* ed. Frank Kermode (London: Routledge, 1960), pp. 55−69, esp. p. 65; and James H. Sims, *The Bible in Milton's Epics* (Gainesville: University of Florida Press, 1962), pp. 259−73 ("Index of Biblical References"). These proposed allusions will be detailed later in the chapter and notes.

Yet so eminent a scholar as Hanford, whose classic study "The Youth of Milton" (1925) recognized the psalmist character of Adam and Eve's garden hymn, did not find "the slightest discernible relation" between the poet's early experience as a psalmist and "such subjective experience as is embodied, for example, in the invocations of *Paradise Lost*" (*John Milton: Poet and Humanist,* p. 8).

The Old Testament prophets, by contrast, have long been studied as appropriate contexts for Milton's life and writings. See, for example, Sir Herbert J. C. Grierson, *Milton and Wordsworth: Poets and Prophets: A Study of Their Reactions to Political Events* (New York: Macmillan, 1937); William Kerrigan, *The Prophetic Milton* (Charlottesville: University Press of Virginia, 1974); and Joseph Anthony Wittreich, Jr., ed., " 'A Poet Amongst Poets': Milton and the Tradition of Prophecy," *Milton and the Line of Vision* (Madison: University of Wisconsin Press, 1975), pp. 97−142.

5. See Hanford, *John Milton: Poet and Humanist,* p. 4.

6. Probably his last literary ambition before his death at Zutphen. See William A. Ringler, Jr., ed., introduction, *The Poems of Sir Philip Sidney* (Oxford: Clarendon Press, 1962), pp. 1−li.

Sidney wrote in *The Defence of Poesie,* published in 1595: "The chiefe [kind of poetry] both in antiquitie and excellencie, were they that did imitate the unconceivable excellencies of God. Such were, *David* in his Psalmes, *Salomon* in his song of songs, in his *Ecclesiastes*, and *Proverbes*, *Moses* and *Debora* in their Hymnes, and the Wryter of *Jobe* . . . against these none will speake that hath the holie Ghost in due holie reverence." From *The Complete Works of Sir Philip Sidney*, ed. Albert Feuillerat, III (Cambridge: Cambridge University Press, 1923), 9.

7. "Reason of Church Government," I, 815−16.

8. See Harris Francis Fletcher, *The Intellectual Development of John Milton* (Urbana: University of Illinois Press, 1956), I, 276−92. "The attention devoted to Hebrew versification in the teaching of Hebrew in Milton's day stands out in any study of that teaching. Because the readings so frequently began with the Psalms, some attention was accorded to Hebrew versification almost as soon as the boy began" (p. 284). Fletcher attempts to reconstruct the complex exercises of translation from Hebrew to Greek to Latin to English that Milton may have performed as a student and speculates that "we actually have two steps in the process from Milton's pen, the English Psalm 114 and its corresponding Greek rendering" (p. 292). Other scholars believe that they were "extracurricular activities" (Clark, p. 183). If they were, of course, Milton's early interest would seem to be even more pronounced. See Donald Lemen Clark, *John Milton at St. Paul's School: A Study of Ancient Rhetoric in English Renaissance Education* (New York: Columbia University Press, 1948), p. 183; and Hanford, *John Milton, Englishman* (New York: Crown, 1949), p. 19.

9. Lawrence E. Toombs, "The Psalms," *The Interpreter's One-Volume Commentary on the Bible*, ed. Charles M. Laymon (New York: Abingdon Press, 1971) p. 256.

10. Toombs, "The Psalms," p. 257.

11. Sirluck, "Milton's Idle Right Hand," pp. 770−71.

William B. Hunter has argued that the later translations of the Psalms were a vital factor in the emergence of the mature prosody of *Paradise Lost*. See his "Sources of Milton's Prosody," *Philological Quarterly*, 27 (1949), 125−44.

12. Milton's translation is here closer to the King James: "Lest he tear my soul like a lion, rending it to pieces, while there is none to deliver" (7:2).

13. Toombs, "The Psalms," p. 257.

14. Interesting as possible rehearsals for specific invocations are "Shine forth, *and from thy cloud give light*" (80:1), "And praise thee *from their loathsom bed / With pale and hollow eyes*" (88:10) for Book III and "Thou in the lowest pit *profound / Hast set me all forlorn*" (88:6) for Book VII (esp. line 20, "forlorne").

15. One of those names, the Tetragrammaton, has long been thought by some biblical commentators to imply the ultimate "namelessness" of God.

Philo Judaeus, in the first century, is usually supposed to have begun this line of commentary.

See Milton's own account of the biblical names of God in *The Christian Doctrine*, Book I, Ch. 2, Yale Edition, VI, 130−52.

16. Letter to Diodati, 1637, Yale Edition, I, 326. Milton here is quoting a line that appears in the conclusion of several of Euripides's plays.

17. As noted in Ch. 3 (n. 2), most of the background research on the epic invocations has been designed to elucidate this very problem—with the implicit faith that traditions outside the poem could best clarify it, but with the final result that the diverse traditions found by scholars could not be reconciled successfully. The use of diverse traditions, however, is exactly what we would expect if my argument is correct.

18. *Saint Augustines Confessions translated: and with some marginall notes illustrated. Wherein, Divers Antiquities are explayned: And the marginall notes of a former Popish Translation, answered.* By William Watts, Rector of St. Albanes, Woodstreete, London, Printed by John Norton, for John Partridge . . . 1631. I. 1−2. (The translation Milton would probably have read, if he read any.)

The possible relevance of this and the following passages to the interrogatory mode of Milton's invocation to light seems to have escaped the notice of previous commentators.

19. See Kenneth Burke, *The Rhetoric of Religion: Studies in Logology* (Boston: Beacon Press, 1961), p. 51.

20. Next to this passage, the seventeenth-century translator William Watts (1631) inserts the marginal note: "Psal. 147.5."

21. See Burke, p. 55.

22. The description of the young Milton as a burner of midnight oil is not fanciful: "From my twelfth year scarcely ever did I leave my studies for my bed before the hour of midnight." *Second Defence of the English People,* (1654), Yale edition, IV, i, 612.

23. The pioneering work is Hanford's "The Youth of Milton" (see n. 2 of this chapter), where he demonstrates: "The aesthetic objectivity of the Horton poems was in considerable degree an artificial thing. Beneath it, and in the entire body of Milton's youthful writing, we may read the evidence of disturbing experiences and intimate reactions which belong characteristically to the period of adolescence." (p. 3).

24. Letter to Diodati, 1637. In this instance, I supply the translation introduced by Hanford (p. 58). It best reveals those qualities of the original that I am seeking to emphasize here.

25. "An Apology Against a Pamphlet" (1642), Yale edition, I, 890.

26. "Reason of Church Government," I, 816−18.

27. "Reason of Church Government," I, 820−21. The last clause seems to confirm our sense of the Nativity Ode's allusion to Isaiah.

28. *A Preface to Paradise Lost* (London: Oxford University Press, 1942), p. 40.

29. Joseph H. Summers, *The Muse's Method*, p. 11.

30. Notice the emphasis of Milton's version when compared with the King James:

> But know that the Lord
> hath set apart him that
> is godly for himself:
> The Lord will hear when
> I call unto him.

(4:3)

31. For other significant variations, see Ps. 11:7, 32:11, 97:11, 125:4, and 112:2.

Daiches ("The Opening of *Paradise Lost*," p. 65) singles out Psalms 15 and 24 for emphasis; Sims (*The Bible in Milton's Epics*, pp. 259 ff.) lists in his general index the following possible allusions to the Psalms that would fall within the lines of the invocations:

PARADISE LOST	PSALMS
I.5	23:3
I.10	2:6
I.12	28:2
I.26	51:4
III.10	104:2
VII.28—29	17:3

32. At the outset, Job is introduced as "perfect and upright" (1:1, 1:8, 2:3) and later one of his "friends" makes the observation quoted in my text. The Book of Job in fact seems almost like the dramatic exposition of a crisis psalm.

Finally, of course, the visionary poet seems to remember the New Testament beatitude: "Blessed are the pure in heart; for they shall see God."

33. The title of the first section (pp. 153—63) of Martz's chapter on Puritanism in *The Poetry of Meditation*.

34. Martz, *Poetry of Meditation*, p. 161. The primary helper in this search was, of course, the Bible—as Martz shows in the example of Bunyan.

35. John Bunyan, *Grace Abounding to the Chief of Sinners*, ed. John Brown (Cambridge: Cambridge University Press, 1907), p. 52; quoted and discussed by Martz, *Poetry of Meditation*, p. 160.

36. Martz, *Poetry of Meditation*, p. 154.

37. Richard Baxter, *The Saints Everlasting Rest*, 4th ed. (London, 1653), part 4; quoted and discussed by Martz, *Poetry of Meditation*, pp. 162—63.

38. Northrop Frye, *The Return of Eden: Five Essays on Milton's Epics* (Toronto: University of Toronto Press, 1965), p. 9.

39. I follow the precedent of Tillyard in calling the *Second Defence* "the greatest of Milton's prose works" (*Milton*, p. 192).

40. *Second Defence*, IV, i, 587.

41. *Second Defence*, IV, i, 548.

42. *Second Defence*, IV, i, 557—58, 558.

43. Milton twice refers to it as "this proem." *Second Defence*, IV, i, 557. Milton, of course, uses the term primarily in the ancient rhetorical sense.

44. *Second Defence*, IV, i, 590.

45. Milton's calling the light "holy" seems to me enriched by the nuance of otherness emphasized in Rudolf Otto's classic account *The Idea of the Holy*, trans. John W. Harvey (London: Oxford University Press, 1923).

46. This idea was suggested to me by Martin Price's comment on Stonehenge as a scene of the sublime: "The evocation is not simply of a power that is wholly other, but the evocation of deep-lying powers within the poet." See his "The Sublime Poem: Pictures and Powers," *The Yale Review*, 58 (1969), 194—213. The possible relevance of Otto's *Idea of the Holy* also was suggested by Price's discussion.

47. "The Crisis of *Paradise Lost*" is the title of Tillyard's chapter on the Fall and Adam and Eve's reconciliation; *Studies in Milton* (London: Chatto and Windus, 1951), pp. 8—52.

48. See Edward Phillips, *Life of Milton*; in Hughes edition, p. 1,035.

49. Maud Bodkin, *Archetypal Patterns in Poetry: Psychological Studies of Imagination* (London: Oxford University Press, 1934), p. 157.

50. The poet's repeated allusions to the Creation (I.9—10, 19—22; III.8—12; VII.5—12) suggest a contrast between the poet as creator and Satan as illusionist. For Satan is ever changing shapes, like Proteus, but he never *becomes* anything other than what he is—doomed, like the cormorant that descends into the Garden, always to be hedging on the Tree of Life.

51. See Harold E. Toliver, "Complicity of Voice in *Paradise Lost*," *Modern Language Quarterly*, 25 (1964), 153—70, esp. 162.

52. Just possibly, Satan's encounter with light on Mount Niphates may be intended to form a paradigmatic contrast to Moses' illumination on the secret top of Sinai, which may then be seen as the common basis of Milton's invocation to light and Satan's anti-invocation. Edward Phillips, Milton's nephew and most reliable early biographer, records how Satan's anti-invocation (composed early) was at one stage designed for the beginning of his "Tragedy" (to become *Paradise Lost*). Thus Milton himself seems to have recognized the invocatory nature of the piece. (See Phillips, *Life of Milton*, pp. 1,034—35). At other stages of the composition, there is a prologue spoken by Moses. See James Holly Hanford, "That Shepherd, Who First Taught the

Chosen Seed: A Note on Milton's Mosaic Inspiration," *University of Toronto Quarterly*, 8 (1938–39), 403–19.

53. Leslie Brisman, *Milton's Poetry of Choice and Its Romantic Heirs* (Ithaca, N.Y., and London: Cornell University Press, 1973), p. 280.

54. The mode of Satan's soliloquy, by contrast, seems like a clever parody of the normal Puritan form of religious meditation. For the Puritan way of meditation resembled a preaching to oneself. "Soliloquy" says Richard Baxter, "is a Preaching to ones self . . . Therefore the very same *Method* which a *Minister* should use in his preaching to others, should a *Christian* use in speaking to himself." Thus Satan self-preaches:

> Hadst thou the same free Will and Power to stand?
> Thou hadst: whom hast thou then or what to accuse,
> But Heav'n's free Love dealt equally to all?
>
> (IV.66–78)

> O then at last relent: is there no place
> Left for Repentance, none for Pardon left?
>
> (79–80)

> For never can true reconcilement grow
> Where wounds of deadly hate have pierc'd so deep
>
> (98–99)

Satan's self-sermonizing climaxes with his farewell to the congregation of his soul—"so farewell Hope, and with Hope farewell Fear, / Farewell Remorse" (lines 108–9)—and a final moral—"Evil be thou my Good" (line 110).

See Baxter, *Saints Everlasting Rest*, quoted and discussed by Martz in *The Poetry of Meditation*, p. 174.

55. Coleridge observed: "Milton has carefully marked in his Satan the intense selfishness, the alcohol of egotism, which would rather reign in hell than serve in heaven. To place this lust of self in opposition to denial of self or duty, and to show what exertions it would make, and what pains endure to accomplish its end, is Milton's particular object in the character of Satan. But around this character he has thrown a singularity of daring, a grandeur of sufferance and a ruined splendor, which constitute the very height of poetic sublimity." From *The Romantics on Milton: Formal Essays and Critical Asides*, ed. Joseph Anthony Wittreich, Jr. (Cleveland: The Press of Case Western University, 1970), p. 244.

56. See Watkins, *Anatomy of Milton's Verse*, pp. 103–4, for a discussion of "unresolved conflicts." On *Paradise Regained* as a "long contest of styles," see Martz, *Paradise Within*, p. 186.

57. Tillyard, *Milton*, p. 306.

58. Tillyard, *Milton*, p. 309. Tillyard speculates that the self-severe

gesture may belong to a mood of disappointment after the Civil War.

59. Tillyard, *Milton*, p. 309.

60. Perhaps this provides some of the animus for Christ's attack on the classics. If so, *Samson Agonistes* may represent a rediscovery and reaffirmation of Greek tragedy as a form capable of expressing this spiritual experience, and thus *Samson* may be viewed as a hard-won and final synthesis of Greek and biblical forms.

61. The title of the preface in the first edition (1671).

My treatment of *Samson* as the last of Milton's works is based, of course, on an assumption honored by tradition and instinct, but questioned by certain modern scholars—questioned, in fact, to such an extent that the most substantial part of the introduction in the Hughes edition (pp. 531—48) concerns not the poem, but the dating of its composition. Yet this long controversy has not only failed to establish a new date, it has not even found a *probable* alternative; in the end "we come back to the view of Masson, Grierson, and Hanford that it was the work of Milton's old age" (Hughes, pp. 539—40)—a position now seemingly confirmed, as such things often are in the modern age, by "statistical comparisons of the frequencies of the strong pauses, feminine endings, and some less interesting prosodic phenomena" (Hughes, p. 540).

62. Preface to *Samson Agonistes;* Columbia Edition, I, ii, 331.

63. Although the poet's voice cannot intervene in drama, we hear its accents firmly in this preface, defending, as did the epic poet, his choice of subject: "Tragedy . . . hath been ever held the gravest, moralest, and most profitable of all other Poems" (as with every true creative spirit, each abyss he broods on is the best one for that moment). "And though antient Tragedy use no Prologue," he intrudes, seemingly aware of his lack of personal voice in the Tragedy, he offers this "self defence, or explanation." But there is no ultimate need for the poet now to intercede in a dramatic world whose first words—Samson's famous soliloquy—so perfectly express and "purge" the "passions" of the poet himself, who seems to say

> here I feel amends,
> The breath of Heav'n fresh-blowing, pure and sweet,
> With day-spring born; here leave me to respire.
>
> (9—11)

64. See Ps. 124:7, for example.

65. The treatment of light in the soliloquy is, of course, reminiscent of the epic invocation to light; in some ways, it is a dramatic reworking of the invocation. In addition, the two passages share an emphasis on light as the "first created Beam" (*Samson*, line 83) and "ofspring of Heav'n first-born" (*Paradise Lost*, III.1).

66. The lamentation motif is pervasive. Other significant examples occur at lines 23, 36, 101, 193, 348, 606, and 1,660.

67. As Dalila knows, his "secrets" are his "key of strength and safety" (lines 798−99). And Samson confesses to her: "I . . . unbosom'd all my secrets to thee" (lines 876−79).

68. *Krinein:* "to cut," "to separate," "to decide."

Selected Bibliography

INVOCATION

Aristotle. *On Interpretation.* Trans. E. M. Edjhill. *The Works of Aristotle, I.* Great Books of the Western World. Ed. R. M. Hutchins. Chicago: Encyclopaedia Britannica, 1952. Vol. VIII.

St. Augustine. *De Trinitate. Later Works.* Trans. John Burnaby. Library of Christian Classics. London: SCM Press, 1955. Vol. VIII.

Baxter, Richard. *The Saints Everlasting Rest.* 4th ed. London, 1653.

Bodkin, Maud. *Archetypal Patterns in Poetry: Psychological Studies of Imagination.* London: Oxford University Press, 1934.

Bunyan, John. *Grace Abounding to the Chief of Sinners.* Ed. John Brown. Cambridge: Cambridge University Press, 1907.

Burke, Kenneth. *The Rhetoric of Religion: Studies in Logology.* Boston: Beacon Press, 1961.

Curtius, Ernst Robert. *European Literature and the Latin Middle Ages.* Trans. Willard R. Trask. Bollingen Series XXXVI. New York: Pantheon Books, 1953.

de Man, Paul. "Symbolic Landscape in Wordsworth and Yeats," in *In Defense of Reading: A Reader's Approach to Literary Criticism.* Eds. Reuben A. Brower and Richard Poirier. New York: Dutton, 1962.

Eliade, Mircea, ed. *From Primitives to Zen: A Thematic Sourcebook of the History of Religions.* New York: Harper and Row, 1967.

————. *Myths, Dreams and Mysteries: The Encounter between Contemporary Faiths and Archaic Realities.* Trans. Philip Mairet. Harper Torchbooks. New York: Harper and Row, 1967.

————. *Shamanism: Archaic Techniques of Ecstasy*. Trans. Willard R. Trask. Bollingen Series LXXVI. Princeton University Press, 1964.

Gardner, Edmund G. *Dante and the Mystics: A Study of the Mystical Aspect of the Divina Commedia and Its Relations with Some of Its Medieval Sources*. London: Dent, 1913.

Hamman, Rev. Adalbert G. "Prayer," *Encyclopaedia Britannica*. 15th ed., 1974.

Harrison, Jane Ellen. *Themis: A Study of the Social Origins of Greek Religion*. Cambridge: Cambridge University Press, 1912.

Havelock, Eric A. *Preface to Plato*. Cambridge, Mass.: Harvard University Press, 1963.

Hesiod. *Theogony*. Trans. Norman O. Brown. The Library of Liberal Arts. Indianapolis: Bobbs-Merrill, 1953.

————. *Theogony*. Trans. H. G. Evelyn-White. Loeb Classical Series. Rev. ed. London: Heinemann, 1936.

Knight, G. Wilson. *The Burning Oracle: Studies in the Poetry of Action*. London: Oxford University Press, 1939.

Macdonell, A. A. "Hymns (Vedic)." *Encyclopaedia of Religion and Ethics*. Ed. James Hastings. New York: Scribner's, 1915. Vol. VII.

Maclean, A. J. "Invocation (Liturgical)." *Encyclopaedia of Religion and Ethics*. Ed. James Hastings. Vol. VII.

Ong, Walter J., S.J. *The Presence of the Word: Some Prolegomena for Cultural and Religious History*. New Haven: Yale University Press, 1967.

Otto, Rudolf. *The Idea of the Holy*. Trans. John W. Harvey. London: Oxford University Press, 1923.

Ovid. *The Art of Love and Other Poems*. Trans. J. H. Mozley. Rev. ed. Cambridge, Mass.: Harvard University Press, 1939.

Pindar. *The Odes of Pindar*. Trans. Richmond Lattimore. Chicago: University of Chicago Press, 1947.

Plato. *Phaedrus*. Trans. B. Jowett. *The Dialogues of Plato*. Great Books of the Western World. Vol. VII.

Price, Martin. "The Sublime Poem: Pictures and Powers," *The Yale Review*, 58 (1969).

Putnam, Michael C. J. *Tibullus: A Commentary*. Norman, Okla.: University of Oklahoma Press, 1973.

Ringler, William A., Jr., ed. Introduction, *The Poems of Sir Philip*

Sidney. Oxford: Clarendon Press, 1962.

Sandys, George. *Ovid's Metamorphosis: Englished, Mythologized, and Represented in Figures*. Eds. K. K. Hulley and S. T. Vandersall. Lincoln: University of Nebraska Press, 1970.

Shaw, Robert Burns. *The Call of God: The Theme of Vocation in Donne, Herbert, and Milton*. Diss. Yale, December 1974.

Sidney, Sir Philip. *The Complete Works of Sir Philip Sidney*. Ed. Albert Feuillerat. Cambridge: Cambridge University Press, 1923. Vol. III.

Tasso, Torquato. *Discourses on the Heroic Poem*. Trans. Mariella Calvalchini and Irene Samuel. New York: Oxford University Press, 1973.

Tibullus. *The Poems of Tibullus*. Trans. Philip Dunlop. Baltimore: Penguin, 1972.

Toombs, Lawrence E. "The Psalms." *The Interpreter's One-Volume Commentary on the Bible*. Ed. Charles M. Laymon. New York: Abingdon Press, 1971.

Vergil. *Georgics*. Trans. H. R. Fairclough. Rev. ed. Cambridge, Mass: Harvard University Press, 1967.

Wissowa, G. "Invocation (Roman)." *Encyclopaedia of Religion and Ethics*. Ed. James Hastings. Vol. VII.

EDITIONS OF MILTON'S WORKS

Complete Prose Works of John Milton. Gen. ed. Don M. Wolfe. 8 vols. New Haven: Yale University Press, 1953—1982.

John Milton: Complete Poems and Major Prose. Ed. Merritt Y. Hughes. New York: Odyssey Press, 1957.

Paradise Lost. Ed. Thomas Newton. London, 1749.

The Poems of John Milton. Eds. John Carey and Alastair Fowler. Longman's Annotated English Poets. London: Longmans, 1968.

The Works of John Milton. Gen. ed. Frank Allen Patterson. 18 vols. New York: Columbia University Press, 1931—38.

LITERARY CRITICISM OF MILTON'S WORKS

Allen, Don Cameron. *The Harmonious Vision: Studies in Milton's Poetry*. Rev. ed. Baltimore: The Johns Hopkins Press, 1970.

Brisman, Leslie. *Milton's Poetry of Choice and Its Romantic Heirs*.

Ithaca, N.Y., and London: Cornell University Press, 1973.

Brooks, Cleanth, and Hardy, J. E., eds. *Poems of Mr. John Milton: The 1645 Edition with Essays in Analysis*. New York: Harcourt, Brace, 1951.

Clark, Donald Lemen. *John Milton at St. Paul's School: A Study of Ancient Rhetoric in English Renaissance Education*. New York: Columbia University Press, 1948.

Coolidge, John S. "Great Things and Small: The Virgilian Progression." *Comparative Literature*, 17 (1965).

Crump, Galbraith Miller. *The Mystical Design of Paradise Lost*. Lewisburg, Pa.: Bucknell University Press, 1975.

Daiches, David. "The Opening of *Paradise Lost*." *The Living Milton*. Ed. Frank Kermode. London: Routledge, 1960.

Delasanta, Rodney. *The Epic Voice*. The Hague: Mouton, 1967.

Ferry, Anne Davidson. *Milton's Epic Voice: The Narrator in Paradise Lost*. Cambridge, Mass.: Harvard University Press, 1963.

Fish, Stanley. *Surprised by Sin: The Reader in Paradise Lost*. London: Macmillan, 1967.

Fletcher, Angus. *The Transcendental Masque: An Essay on Milton's Comus*. Ithaca, N.Y., and London: Cornell University Press, 1971.

Fletcher, Harris Francis. *The Intellectual Development of John Milton*. 2 vols. Urbana: University of Illinois Press, 1956.

Frye, Northrop. *The Return of Eden: Five Essays on Milton's Epics*. Toronto: University of Toronto Press, 1965.

Greene, Thomas. *The Descent from Heaven: A Study in Epic Continuity*. New Haven: Yale University Press, 1963.

Grierson, Sir Herbert. *Milton and Wordsworth: Poets and Prophets: A Study of Their Reactions to Political Events*. New York: Macmillan, 1937.

Hanford, James Holly. *John Milton, Englishman*. New York, Crown, 1949.

————. *John Milton: Poet and Humanist*. Cleveland: The Press of Western Reserve University, 1966.

————. "That Shepherd, Who First Taught the Chosen Seed: A Note on Milton's Mosaic Inspiration." *University of Toronto Quarterly*, 8 (1938–39).

————. "The Youth of Milton: An Interpretation of His Early Literary Development." *University of Michigan Studies in*

Shakespeare, Milton and Donne. New York, Macmillan, 1925.

Hollander, John. *The Untuning of the Sky: Ideas of Music in English Poetry, 1500−1700.* Princeton: Princeton University Press, 1961.

Hughes, Merritt Y. "Milton and the Symbol of Light." *Studies in English Literature 1500−1900,* 4 (1964). Rpt. in his *Ten Perspectives on Milton.* New Haven: Yale University Press, 1965.

Hunter, William B. "Sources of Milton's Prosody," *Philological Quarterly,* 27 (1949).

Johnson, Samuel. *Lives of the English Poets.* Ed. George Birkbeck Hill. 3 vols. Oxford: Clarendon Press, 1905.

Kerrigan, William. *The Prophetic Milton.* Charlottesville: University Press of Virginia, 1974.

Lewis, C. S. *A Preface to Paradise Lost.* London: Oxford University Press, 1942.

Lord, George deF. "Milton's Dialogue with Omniscience." *The Author in His Work: Essays on a Problem in Criticism.* Ed. Louis L. Martz and Aubrey Williams. New Haven: Yale University Press, 1978.

MacCaffrey, Isabel Gamble, ed. Introduction. *John Milton: Samson Agonistes and the Shorter Poems.* The Signet Classical Poetry Series. New York: The New American Library, 1966.

————. *Paradise Lost as "Myth."* Cambridge, Mass.: Harvard University Press, 1959.

Martz, Louis L. *The Paradise Within: Studies in Vaughan, Traherne, and Milton.* New Haven: Yale University Press, 1964.

————. *The Poetry of Meditation: A Study in English Relgious Literature of the Seventeenth Century.* New Haven: Yale University Press, 1954.

————. "The Rising Poet, 1645." *The Lyric and Dramatic Milton.* English Institute Essays. Ed. Joseph H. Summers. New York: Columbia University Press, 1965.

Mayerson, Caroline W. "The Orpheus Image in *Lycidas.*" *PMLA,* 64 (1949).

Phillips, Edward. *Life of Milton.* Hughes edition.

Prince, F. T. *The Italian Element in Milton's Verse.* Oxford: Clarendon Press, 1954.

Sims, James H. *The Bible in Milton's Epics.* Gainesville: University of

Florida Press, 1962.

Riggs, William G. *The Christian Poet in Paradise Lost.* Berkeley: University of California Press, 1972.

Samuel, Irene. *Dante and Milton: The Commedia and Paradise Lost.* Ithaca, N.Y.: Cornell University Press, 1966.

Shawcross, John T. "The Metaphor of Inspiration in Paradise Lost." *Th' Upright Heart and Pure: Essays on John Milton Commemorating the Tercentenary of the Publication of Paradise Lost.* Ed. Amadeus P. Fiore, O.F.M. Pittsburgh: Duquesne University Press, 1967.

Sirluck, Ernest. "Milton's Idle Right Hand." *Journal of English and Germanic Philology,* 60 (1961).

Smith, Hallett. "No Middle Flight." *Huntington Library Quarterly,* 15 (1951 − 52).

Summers, Joseph H. *The Muse's Method: An Introduction to Paradise Lost.* London: Chatto and Windus, 1962.

Svendsen, Kester. "Milton's *L'Allegro* and *Il Penseroso.*" *The Explicator,* 8, No. 49 (1950).

Tillyard, E. M. W. *Milton.* London: Chatto and Windus, 1930.
————. *Studies in Milton.* London: Chatto and Windus, 1951.

Toliver, Harold E. "Complicity of Voice in Paradise Lost." *Modern Language Quarterly,* 25 (1964).

Watkins, W. B. C. *An Anatomy of Milton's Verse.* Baton Rouge: Louisiana State University Press, 1955.

Wittreich, Joseph Anthony, Jr., ed. "A Poet Amongst Poets: Milton and the Tradition of Prophecy." *Milton and the Line of Vision.* Madison: University of Wisconsin Press, 1975.
————. ed. *The Romantics on Milton: Formal Essays and Critical Asides.* Cleveland: The Press of Case Western University, 1970.

Index